AISD

Language Arts

Please return

# 21st Century DISCIPLINE

*Teaching students*
*responsibility and self-control*

By Jane Bluestein, Ph.D.

Instructor Books

12 11 10 9 8 7 6 5 4 3 2                    2 3 4 5/9
Printed in the U.S.A.                               34

Author,Jane Bluestein; Editor, Christine Van Huysse; Designer, Laurie Semmens; Copy editors, Cheryl Brady, Annette Keeler, John Nemec; Production Managers, Jeanne Johnson, Andrea Junker; Director,  Ben Miyares; Manager, Barbara Michel.

SCHOLASTIC INC.
2931 EAST MCCARTY STREET,
JEFFERSON CITY, MO 65102

# Contents

# Preface

A few years ago, after meeting the student teachers and first-year teaching interns I was to supervise, I asked them about the topics and areas of concern they wanted to work on. The question was barely out of my mouth before I heard a unanimous response: Discipline. They had dozens of questions, mostly about how to get students to do something—or stop doing something. *What if they don't listen? What if there's a fight? What if they won't do their work? What if ...?*

Since then, I have run across thousands of teachers whose questions and primary concerns have sounded remarkably similar. Over the years I have discovered few simple answers to the questions about specific behaviors—or misbehaviors. It has been necessary instead to back up and talk about issues such as goals, needs, relationships, cooperation, motivation, success, classroom climate, and responsibility. Without information on these issues, much advice is short-term, often ineffective, and presents solutions out of context to the classroom and the relationships in which the problems occur.

In context, however, discipline becomes a set of preventive techniques that actually encourage student self-management and self-control while reducing the number of conflicts described by the vast majority of *what-if* questions.

My second discovery was the fact that any discussion of student behavior ultimately leads back to teacher behavior. Motivating cooperation from our students usually means modifying our behaviors, learning new interaction skills, and letting go of ineffective or destructive techniques.

This news can be disconcerting; it is always easier to want the other person to change. Even with firm commitments to positive interaction strategies, avoiding the pitfalls of our own negative programming is always a challenge. Keep in mind that learning to motivate students to adjust their behavior is a process on every level—not just for you, but for your students as well.

It may seem confusing or overwhelming, but let's start with where you are. A pre-assessment follows to help you examine your beliefs and the behaviors that are working for you, as well as those that may be keeping you from reaching your goals. As you read through this book, explore and practice new skills and frequently take time to reflect on the progress you are making.

And always, best wishes for continued success and happiness throughout your journey.

Jane Bluestein
July 1988
Albuquerque, New Mexico

# Pre-Assessment

In each pair of statements below, mark the one you identify with most strongly. The sole purpose of this activity is to establish a basis for tracking your own growth and development.

_____ I try to build a positive emotional climate in the classroom.
_____ I prefer to focus on academics. The students are there to learn.

_____ I try to give each student a chance to feel successful by meeting his or her individual needs.
_____ All students have an opportunity to feel successful if they listen and stay caught up.

_____ Whether or not my students cooperate, I communicate my acceptance of them as people.
_____ When my students cooperate, I communicate my approval.

_____ It is possible to have fun with your students and still keep their attention.
_____ Students will probably take advantage of a teacher who tries to have fun with them.

_____ I have a variety of classroom materials out and available for my students to take as needed.
_____ Most of the time, I dispense materials.

_____ I want my students to be cooperative.
_____ I want my students to be obedient.

_____ I may not accept a student's misbehavior, but I can still accept the student.
_____ I cannot accept a student who is misbehaving.

_____ I want my students to listen to me, and I try to make it need-fulfilling for them to do so.
_____ I want my students to listen to me, and I punish them when they do not.

_____ Students can choose responsibly and still not choose what I would like.
_____ I am reluctant to let my kids make decisions because they might not choose what I want them to.

_____ I allow students to experience the natural consequences of misbehavior.
_____ Misbehavior should be punished.

_____ *Johnny, you really got ready in a hurry today!*
_____ *I like the way Johnny got ready today!*

_____ My students are cooperative because they choose to be.
_____ My students are cooperative because I do not allow them to misbehave.

_____ My students can manage OK even if I am not there.
_____ My students behave as long as I do not turn my back on them.

_____ I treat my students the way I would like to be treated.
_____ I really have to blow up at my students from time to time.

_____ *Please put the lid on the paste so it won't dry out.*
_____ *Please put the lid on the paste because I said so.*

_____ I try to find something positive to say about every paper I get.
_____ Students will not learn if you do not correct their mistakes.

_____ I try to speak to my students the way I like to be spoken to.
_____ I sometimes talk to my students in ways I would never speak to another adult.

_____ My students know I care about them even if they are driving me crazy.
_____ I cannot accept my students when they act up.

_____ I like my job most of the time.
_____ I dislike my job most of the time.

_____ I like to call parents when my students are doing well.
_____ I rarely call parents unless my students really mess up.

_____ I give my students reasons for doing things.
_____ Students should do what they are told, period.

_____ I work for my students' respect.
_____ Students should respect me because I am their teacher.

_____ It is possible for students to have power in the classroom without disrupting the class or hurting anyone.
_____ Give them an inch and they will take a yard.

_____ I have immediate consequences for misbehavior.

_____ I frequently give my students warnings and reminders when they misbehave.

_____ I know I am doing a great job when I am prepared and doing my best.

_____ I know I am doing a great job when my students are busy learning.

_____ When my students behave, it is because they are working for positive consequences.

_____ When my students behave, it is because they want to avoid punishment.

_____ Even the best teacher is limited as to what he or she can control.

_____ A teacher should control his or her classroom.

_____ Everyone works better when there is a payoff.

_____ Students should not have to be rewarded for good behavior or performance.

_____ My students find cooperation personally rewarding.

_____ My students want to please me.

_____ I like to joke with my students.

_____ I rarely joke with my students.

_____ I want my students to care about me.

_____ I do not care if my students like me as long as they behave and do their work.

_____ I encourage my students to help with administrative details.

_____ I take care of most of the administrative details in my classroom.

_____ I like to let my students check their own work.

_____ I rarely allow my students access to my answer keys.

_____ I sometimes ask my students to choose which assignments they would like to do first.

_____ My students do their work in a specific sequence.

_____ My students sometimes choose which problems or assignments they want to do.

_____ I determine the assignments for my students.

_____ I sometimes ask my students for input about topics or concepts they want to study.
_____ I determine what we cover in my classroom.

_____ *You can go out for recess as soon as you finish your work.*
_____ *If you don't get your work done, you won't be able to go to recess.*

_____ *If you're quiet in the hall, we'll be able to get to lunch quickly.*
_____ *If you're noisy in the hall, we'll have to come back here.*

_____ *Please pick up those marbles so that no one will slip and fall.*
_____ *Would you pick up those marbles for me, please?*

_____ I try very hard to treat my students with respect, even when I am responding to their negative behavior.
_____ It is sometimes necessary to criticize or humiliate a student.

_____ I have a number of unrelated, non-destructive diversions to relieve work-related stress.
_____ Most of my out-of-school time is devoted to my work.

The first statement in each pair reflects the discipline philosophy described in this book. If you have checked most of these statements, this book will help you enhance what you're already doing. The second statement in the pair reflects an authoritarian or power focus in dealing with children. Read on; you may find more positive alternatives. If you had a difficult time choosing between two statements, this book can point out the differences between the two discipline strategies, which are very different and generally exclusive of one another.

# Introduction

My interest in classroom discipline began before I ever encountered my first group of students; its roots were ignorance and sheer terror. My training (and confidence) had been geared to lesson plans, bulletin boards, and color-coded task cards. In terms of preparation, I could not have been outdone. Yet the thought of facing a roomful of children somehow was not relieved by my skill with the laminator. Throughout my methods courses one question persistently nagged: *But what do I do with the kids?*

I did not get many answers, and those I did hear were not particularly satisfying. More often than not my question was answered with a warning: *Keep them busy and make sure you look like you're in charge.*

Great.

At the time, the university stressed freedom and creativity in the classroom. The undercurrent from the schools, however, warned that control was the goal. To that end, some veterans confessed to having students copy their science books because, when observed, the kids were quiet and looked busy. Is that what I wanted? Was there a way to strike a balance between nurturer and storm trooper?

I went into my classroom with the best bulletin boards in the district and a handful of clichés: Be tough. Be consistent. Be clever. Don't smile before Christmas.

Yet, a few months into the year, I realized there was something missing and spent the next several years looking for the magic that got kids moving, kept them busy, attracted their attention, and generated responsible, caring attitudes and behaviors.

Those few months in the classroom were painful, to say the least. My power was, for the most part, unimpressive and unheeded. My students, though equipped with street smarts and savvy, could not make simple decisions or get from one side of the room to the other without direction. I was so busy nagging, reminding, and policing that I never seemed to do any teaching.

During that time, I learned that love, dedication, and my own creativity would not be enough. I learned that expectations alone do not generate cooperation, that power alienates and ultimately impedes growth, and that heeding the advice not to smile left little room to enjoy being a teacher.

But I also learned that there are tricks that work most of the time, with most of the kids; and the success of these tricks is closely tied to the atmosphere created and the interactions that occur. I slowly discovered alternatives to blaming other teachers, the system, or parents, and eventually found ways to meet students' needs without sacrificing my own.

This book is dedicated to sharing what I have learned, to looking at which teacher behaviors work best in which situations, to encouraging student commitment and responsibility, and to creating a quiet, positive, and preventive discipline structure so that teaching time is spent as it was intended.

# Section One

# You and Your Students

# 1 What you want

efore talking about the whys and hows of discipline and classroom management, let's make sure we are headed in the same direction.

Right now, it's fantasy time. Imagine you have an ideal class of perfect students who behave exactly the way you want, all the time. How do they act? Think about those classroom behaviors that you perceive as ideal. Consider what you want and need as a classroom teacher. Then focus on what your kids want or need in their roles as students in the class.

Regardless of how your students actually behave, imagine each statement in the list on the following page as behavior that you can indeed elicit. If you could have anything you want, how strongly would you want to see the behavior in each statement for the students' benefit and yours?

Use the following scale to complete the survey.

5 = Yes, very much! (Where do I sign up?)
3 = Not crucial, but would be nice.
1 = No big deal.

I want my students to:

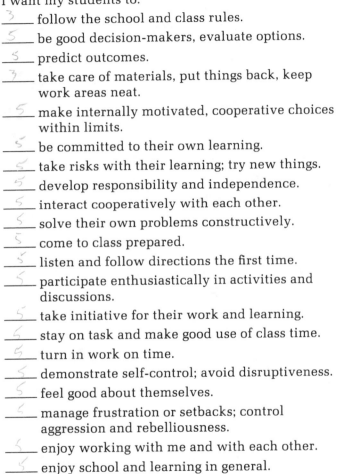

_3_ follow the school and class rules.

_5_ be good decision-makers, evaluate options.

_5_ predict outcomes.

_3_ take care of materials, put things back, keep work areas neat.

_5_ make internally motivated, cooperative choices within limits.

_5_ be committed to their own learning.

_5_ take risks with their learning; try new things.

_5_ develop responsibility and independence.

_5_ interact cooperatively with each other.

_5_ solve their own problems constructively.

_5_ come to class prepared.

_5_ listen and follow directions the first time.

_5_ participate enthusiastically in activities and discussions.

_5_ take initiative for their work and learning.

_5_ stay on task and make good use of class time.

_5_ turn in work on time.

_5_ demonstrate self-control; avoid disruptiveness.

_5_ feel good about themselves.

_5_ manage frustration or setbacks; control aggression and rebelliousness.

_5_ enjoy working with me and with each other.

_5_ enjoy school and learning in general.

Now total your scores. If your score is low (that is, closer to 20 than 100), either your discipline goals are significantly different from those expressed in this book or your imagination was not adequately cranked (try again—be good to yourself!). In either case, consider the following: you have the choice of accomplishing your instructional goals either by spending your time engaged positively (teaching, observing, recognizing) or negatively (nagging, threatening, criticizing).

Which do you choose?

The statements in the list present a definition of discipline that will be used throughout this book. When your students are exhibiting these behaviors, class time can be devoted to instruction and positive interactions. These behaviors do not evolve in a vacuum, however, and the remainder of this book is devoted to helping you create the kind of classroom environment in which students follow rules, come prepared, interact cooperatively, act responsibly, feel good about themselves, and remember to put the caps back on the markers!

The position presented in this book is that discipline is more than simply getting kids to do what you want. The behaviors described in the list are important because when your kids exhibit them your job will be significantly easier and more pleasant. More importantly, students who acquire these skills tend to function more successfully outside the classroom and later in life.

For most of us, however, it is much easier to agree that these behaviors are important and valuable than it is to actually bring them about.

In fact, in many instances, those of us devoted to encouraging independence, responsibility, cooperation, prosocial behaviors, and all of the other skills described above may inadvertently choose teaching behaviors and interactive strategies that actually prevent these skills from developing.

The next chapter examines how we fall into this trap. The rest of the book shows the way out.

# 2 The discipline trap: catching up to the 21st century

**R**emember the television family sitcoms of the 1950s? Regardless of the show, the family structures and values were remarkably alike, reflecting those of suburban, middle-class America at the peak of the postwar industrial era. To a great extent, these values were products of the factory economy. During this period, uniformity was the goal; innovation and initiative were seen as threatening.

These values were clear in the workplace and the classroom, where authority relationships were typically power-oriented. Competitive goal structures limited the number of people who could succeed and behavior was governed by fairly rigid expectations. In the industrial era, one could sometimes get ahead through obedience, dedication, persistence, and the ability to avoid making waves.

With the continuing technological developments of the past few decades, America has changed from an industrial to an information society. This new economy demands a different set of work skills, such as interaction, innovation, negotiation, and communication[1]. With a need for different work skills comes a gradual shift in what is valued in the workplace. While the worker of the industrial age may have looked for security and permanence, workers in the current economy show a marked preference for individuality, personal empowerment, and potential for growth.

That's the good news.

The bad news is that our systems of education are still, for the most part, set up to crank out factory workers. While present-day businesses lean more toward networking, cooperation, negotiation, flexibility, creativity, and divergence, students schooled in a system that values factory-era skills may have difficulty making the transition to an information-age workplace. Even when individual teachers recognize these needs and make a commitment to build toward the future, we are so much a product of win-lose, competitive goal structures that our teaching may lack consistency between well-intentioned goals and our ability to carry them out.

For example, many of us have vowed, at one time or another, never to act or talk like an authoritarian teacher we did not like when we were in school. How many of us have actually kept that promise? Part of the problem is that the person whose behavior we disliked was one of our role models. We grew up with this behavior; and, though it might be difficult to admit, we may have modeled our teaching behavior after this person's because it's familiar.

The value system of the industrial era seeped into all authority relationships. This value system shaped the behavior of our parents and teachers, who used strategies necessary to bring us into a factory society. The model was rigid and power-oriented, operating on a *should, for-your-own-good* mentality and the belief that control and punishment were ultimately effective.

It is doubtful that these parents, teachers, or employers were deliberately abusive; more likely, they were unskilled in the interactive dimensions of their roles and believed themselves to be short on options. Whether or not they actually liked the model, most people accepted and followed the precedents set by their parents, teachers, and bosses, probably without much thought. In this context, information-age priorities, such as individuality, independence, intrinsic motivation, and self-control, could pose a threat to an autocratic, conformity-oriented value system.

If we grew up with power-based, win-lose authority relationships, the behaviors we observed are the ones we tend to adopt. When we apply industrial-age techniques, we interfere with our students' opportunities to develop the skills they will need in an environment structured on a different set of needs and values—often the very skills we are trying to inspire. One problem for many of us is that we learned power-oriented values as we grew up, but through training or experience have adopted more positive goals. Therein lies the confusion and frustration.

*21st century discipline* **means taking time to learn new behaviors to teach responsible learning skills.**

When everything is going along well, we have no need to fear the demons of our upbringing. It is the conflict situation that elicits the words and behaviors we had sworn to avoid. And conflict situations are inevitable when we attempt to motivate or teach skills to information-age children with industrial-age strategies.

Discrepancies can exist between what we are familiar with and what we want. *21st century discipline* means taking time to learn new behaviors to teach responsible learning skills. It means developing techniques to avoid creating conflict in the first place, as well as learning to deal more effectively with conflicts when they arise. In some instances, it also means letting go of industrial-era values that are no longer effective, or even restructuring entire relationships in order to achieve desired results.

Fortunately, the means to reaching these goals are specific, learnable skills that work in and outside the classroom for children and adults. You probably already know many of these skills and use them in successful adult relationships. Now, with the 21st century fast approaching, we have a context for applying them in the classroom.

---

[1] For more information about the change from an industrial society to an information society, read John Naisbitt's *Megatrends*, Warner Books, New York, 1982.

# Industrial Age

**Values,
Priorities,
and Motivators**

- Uniformity, sameness.
- Stability, permanence, security (rigid roles, expectations).
- Competition.
- Motivation for cooperation: external (pleasing authority, avoiding punishment), oriented to teacher.
- Outcome/product orientation.
- Pleasing others, regardless of personal needs.

**Skills**

- Follow orders, obedience.
- Listen.
- Maintain hierarchy, power structure.
- Not making waves, status quo.
- Dependence on leader (credit or blame).

**Authority
Relationships**

- Power-oriented.
- Win-Lose.
- Teacher makes rules, sets limits; enforces.
- Purpose for rules power-based—*Because I said so.*
- Teacher responsible for student's behavior.
- Tendency to take student's misbehavior personally.
- Rescuing behavior is common.

**Discipline Goal:
Controlling
Students**

- Students make few decisions, few opportunities to act independently.
- Independence seen as threatening to power relationship, undermines teacher's role as disciplinarian.
- Punishment for infractions.
- Focus on student's worth.
- Critical; focus on negative.
- Praise for teacher-pleasing behavior.
- Greater rigidity and uniformity in assignments, rewards; evaluation tends to be comparative (based on performance of others).

# Information Age

- Growth potential, personal fulfillment.
- Flexibility, choices, personal control (variable roles).
- Cooperative.
- Motivation for cooperation: internal (emphasis on internal payoff, self-pleasing consequence), oriented to student.
- Process/person orientation.
- Self-care; doing for others with regard to personal needs.

**Values, Priorities, and Motivators**

- Take initiative, make decisions within limits of rules.
- Communicate.
- Network, negotiate.
- Take risks, try new things, innovate.
- Assume personal responsibility, independence.

**Skills**

- Goal/consequence-oriented.
- Win-Win.
- Teacher makes rules, sets limits; encourages self-enforcement.
- Purpose for rules consequence-based, explained to students.
- Students responsible for own behavior.
- Greater detachment from personal impact (without loss of caring).
- Students allowed to experience non-life-threatening consequences of poor choosing.

**Authority Relationships**

- Students have opportunities to make decisions, act independently.
- Independence seen as supporting cooperative relationship; frees teacher for instruction.
- Consequence for infractions.
- Focus on student's behavior.
- Recognition; focus on positive.
- Recognition for performance (not worth).
- Greater divergence and flexibility in assignments, rewards, evaluation, based on individual performance and capability.

**Discipline Goal: Controlling Students**

**Reflection**   Look at the lists on the pages. Then respond to the
following questions.

In what ways did your own experiences as a student
reflect the values, skills, and relationships of the Industrial
Age?

In what ways did your own experiences as a student
reflect the values, skills, and relationships of the
Information Age?

In what ways have your experiences affected your values
and priorities as a teacher?

How do your teaching behaviors reflect your values and
priorities?

What do you want out of teaching? What needs does
teaching fulfill for you? What *can* teaching fulfill for you?

Becoming more effective in our interactions with students involves a number of processes: clarifying goals, examining our own habits and values, and learning and applying new behaviors. The activities presented throughout this book will help direct you on this journey.

# 3     The obedient student

Talk to any nostalgic veteran and you are likely to hear about the good old days when teachers were respected just for being teachers, when children were obedient and easy to control, and when the threat of a bad grade or a phone call home could often keep the worst of the lot in line.

It is true that teacher-student relationships are not the same as they were a generation ago. A child's world is larger today than it was in the past; there is greater mobility and access to more resources and information than ever before, and children have more responsibility and independence at an earlier age. While their basic needs are the same as children in times past, the means for satisfying these needs have changed and motivators and deterrents that were effective in the past may not work with them.

Using the autocratic, competitive strategies of factory-era management appears effective, but the results are inconsistent with the values and demands of our information-oriented society. Obedience may have been the ultimate discipline goal of the industrial age. However, in the information era, it is possible for students to actually be too obedient.

**There is evidence that children who are too obedient may have difficulty functioning in today's work world.**

We assume that a good teacher is one whose students listen and do as they are told—the more obedient the children, the better the reflection on the teacher. And we have been raised to believe that the obedient child is the one best able to assume his or her place as a responsible member of society. While that assumption may have held true in an industrial society, there is a great deal of evidence that children who are too obedient may have difficulty functioning as independent, responsible individuals in today's work world.

And yet, to some, the idea of questioning the sanctity of obedience stirs visions of anarchy, or at least, permissiveness. 21st century discipline, however, is not remotely in favor of either. Your classroom, and every group or institution, needs rules and limits in order to function. And to function effectively requires cooperation within those limits.

So the question is not whether to have rules, but, what is the best way to motivate cooperation? To answer, let's first look at the difference between obedience and cooperation.

On the outside they look the same. For example, your supervisor has planned to observe your class later today. You know she is a stickler for time on task so you want to keep your second graders busy.

Just before she is scheduled to arrive, you take one group aside and say, *Now listen. If you don't do your work, you can forget about recess for the rest of your lives.* These students live for playground time; they get busy.

You take the next group aside and coo, *You know, boys and girls, I just love it when you finish your work for me.*[1] You know this group, too. Your love and approval is very important; they get right down to work.

The kids in group three are TV addicts: *If your work is done by 2:00, you may watch the show on jungle animals.* They get right down to work.

Your supervisor comes in and what does she see? Everyone is busy working. The outcome behavior is obvious; the motivation is not.

The first group complies because the students are more attached to their free time than to not doing the work. This is an example of motivating through fear. The strategy carries with it the threat of deprivation (in this case, loss of recess), or, in other situations, of punishment or even physical consequences.

The students in group two want you to care about them more than they want to avoid doing their work so they comply. This, too, is an example of motivation through fear, only here it is fear of the withdrawal of approval or affection that elicits the response.

The students in the third group probably did not find the assignments any more compelling than the rest of the class, but they did want to watch that show. In the first two examples, the students obey to avoid the teacher's wrath or gain approval. Their motivation is *external*; the consequence of group three's cooperation is not. Their motivation is *based on their needs* and is *internal*.

If you are wondering, *What difference does it make—the teacher got what she wanted and so did the kids?*, put yourself in the place of the student. Which motivation would you prefer? And, as a teacher, given the choice of motivators, which would you prefer that your students respond to?

Obedience is externally motivated by fear of punishment, pain, abandonment or deprivation. Affection and caring can be dangerous, particularly if offered only when the student is doing what the teacher wants. This is *conditional* love. In whatever form it is expressed, it implies conditional rejection and can be punitive and fear-producing.

In contrast, responsible cooperation characterizes 21st century discipline. It is internally motivated, a positive consequence to a positive choice. There are a number of reasons why this option is preferable to the former, even if each appears to achieve the same short-term outcome.

**Responsible cooperation characterizes *21st century discipline.* It is internally motivated, a positive consequence to a positive choice.**

Perhaps the most benign consequence of obedience is evident from a common complaint from teachers of obedient students: *Sure they do what I tell them, but that's ALL they do!* These children are so used to doing what they are told that they are likely to wait for instructions and then take them literally.

A kindergarten teacher discovered three bewildered students wandering around the room with their hands full of scraps because she had told them to pick them up, without elaborating about throwing the scraps in the trash can. When an entire group of fifth-grade students forgot to use capital letters in a punctuation review, the teacher, they claimed, was to blame: *You didn't remind us.* These students were *not* independent thinkers!

Because so much external validation and approval is tied to obedience—we reinforce with praise and affection those behaviors that we want—children become conditioned to believe that they are good and worthwhile only when they are pleasing someone else. This tendency may be hard to avoid. Let's face it—as teachers, we love to be pleased now and then. But if we give positive feedback to students only when they do what we want, we are, inadvertently, conditioning them to become people-pleasers, to think of the needs of others before or instead of their own.

It is possible that in certain situations or groups these students might lose their ability to think and act in their own best interests, and endanger or compromise their safety, health or happiness. As long as you are the one doing the ordering and reinforcing, there may be no problem; after all, you have your students' safety and well-being at heart. But obedient children will obey anyone whose love and approval is important to them. (Watch your students as peer pressure gains importance in their lives.)

Such children may have difficulty making decisions because they do not know who they are and what they really want, and this trait is likely to be carried into adulthood. By defining themselves from an external frame of reference, their self-images are at the mercy of anyone with whom they interact. These factors reinforce dependence, low self-confidence, and poor self-esteem, regardless of the praise we offer.

**The authority relationship that encourages obedience reinforces victim behavior, powerlessness, and rebelliousness.**

Because children raised with *Do as you're told!* do not have many opportunities to make decisions, they may also have difficulty solving problems and anticipating the probable outcome of the choices they make. Obedient children may have difficulty accepting responsibility for their choices; they are more likely to blame forces outside of themselves for anything good or bad that occurs in their lives. How often do you hear, *It wasn't my fault, he started it*, or *She made me do it*? One high school teacher related a conversation in which a student expelled for arson claimed, *Hey, I just lit the match. I didn't know the building would burn down.*

Finally, obedience is generally a win-lose proposition that depends upon the powerlessness of the person who obeys. The authority relationship that encourages obedience reinforces victim behavior, powerlessness, and limitations, or provokes rebelliousness. Thus, obedient children tend to face life with a narrow range of responses to negative situations: continue to suffer or hurt someone else.

Obedience is often a deterrent to responsibility and independence. While this reality may appear grim—or at least unnerving—take heart. It *is* possible to get the same kind of cooperation that obedience promises and to build responsible learning and living skills along the way!

As adults working with children, teachers are in an excellent position to help students acquire the tools for thinking and deciding, to encourage personal empowerment with regard to rules, limits, and the needs of others, and to inspire a positive self-concept, based not on the opinions of others, but on self-knowledge and confidence.

---

[1] In case it is not obvious, these examples are offered to make a point and are neither recommended nor suggested as motivational strategies.

# The Obedient Student

**Characteristics**

- Motivated by external factors, such as the need to please authority and experience extrinsic approval.
- Follows orders.
- May lack confidence in ability to function in absence of authority; lacks initiative; waits for orders.
- Self-esteem: defined externally— worthwhile when getting approval.
- *I am my behavior* (and somebody else probably made me this way).
- Difficulty seeing connection between behavior and consequence.
- Difficulty seeing options or choices; difficulty making decisions.
- Helplessness and teacher-dependence common.
- Operates from external value system (often that of someone important to him/her) that may not be personally relevant and could be harmful.
- Obeys, may think.
- Lacks confidence in personal instincts and ability to act in own self-interest.
- Difficulty predicting outcomes or consequences.
- Difficulty understanding or expressing personal needs.
- Limited ability to get needs met without hurting self or others.
- Limited negotiation skills; orientation is You win-I lose.
- Compliant.
- Commitment to avoid punishment, *keeping teacher off my back.*
- May experience conflict between internal and external needs (what I want vs. what teacher wants); may experience guilt or rebelliousness.
- May make poor choices to avoid disapproval or abandonment (*to make my friends like me more.*)

# The Responsible Student*

- Motivated by internal factors, such as the need to weigh choices and experience personal consequences.
- Makes choices.
- More confident in ability to function in absence of authority; takes initiative.
- Self-esteem: defined internally—worthwhile with or without approval (or even with disapproval).
- *I am not my behavior, although I am responsible for how I behave.*
- Better able to see the connection between behavior and consequence.
- Better able to see options or choices, able to make decisions.
- Personal empowerment and independence common.
- Operates from internal value system (what is best or safest for him/her), considering needs and values of others.
- Thinks, may obey.
- Confidence in personal instincts and ability to act in own self-interest.
- Better able to predict outcomes or consequences.
- Better able to understand and express personal needs.
- Better able to get own needs without hurting self or others.
- Better-developed negotiation skills; orientation is You win-I win.
- Cooperative.
- Commitment to task, experiencing outcome of positive choosing.
- Better able to resolve conflict between internal and external needs (what I want vs. what teacher wants); less inclined toward guilt or rebelliousness.
- May make poor choices to experience personal consequences and to satisfy curiosity.

**Characteristics**

# Teacher Behaviors, Beliefs, and Attitudes

**Encourage Obedience**

- Judgmental, authoritative, critical.
- Often inconsistent; likely to have double standard for adult and student behaviors.
- Outcome-oriented.
- Criteria for choices offered based on teacher power: *Because I TOLD you.* Demands.
- Orders, tells; the choices offered to students are rarely more than *do it or else.*
- Likely to mistrust student's ability to decide in own best interest; may mistrust student's motivation.
- Makes decision for the student: *I know what's best for you.*
- Offers few opportunities for student to practice decision-making.
- States contingencies negatively (as threats): *If you don't . . . .*
- Punishment-oriented.
- Teacher's needs more important than student's needs.
- Likely to be threatened by student's independence and initiative; may discourage or prevent both types of behavior. Protective; has difficulty allowing student to experience negative consequences of poor decisions or mistakes; more likely to cover for student's poor choosing; inclined toward rescuing.
- Takes responsibility for student's behavior and consequences: If student forgets library book, *I have to remind you every week.*

# Teacher Behaviors, Beliefs, and Attitudes

**Encourage Responsibility**

- More positive orientation to students.

- Tries to be consistent; tries to model behaviors (for adults and students).

- Process-oriented.

- Criteria for choices offered based on consequences: *If you put the caps back on the markers, they won't be dried out next time.*

- Requests, asks; choices are task-oriented.

- Trusts student's ability to make decisions; likely to understand that student is motivated by own needs.

- Avoids making decisions for student; will give student information and encourage decision-making based on that information; guides, helps.

- Can still feel needed by independent student; encourages independence and initiative.

- States contingencies positively (promises): *If you do . . .*

- Reward-oriented.

- Teacher's needs are equally important to student's needs.

- May have difficulty allowing student to experience negative consequences but willing to allow student to make and learn from mistakes (except in life-threatening situations); resists inclination to rescue.

- Leaves responsibility for student's behavior and consequences with student: Student forgets library book because of poor decision made by student.

* All the charts in this book adapted from *Parents In A Pressure Cooker*, Bluestein & Collins, Programs for Education, Rosemount, NJ, 1988.

**Reflection**    Look at the descriptions of the obedient student and the responsible student.

In what ways are the characteristics of the obedient student consistent with the behaviors you would like to encounter or encourage in your own students?

Are there any characteristics that concern you? For what reason?

In what ways are the characteristics of the responsible student consistent with the behaviors you would like to encounter or encourage in your own students?

Are there any characteristics that concern you? For what reason?

From a personal standpoint, to which characteristics do you best relate?

What have been the positive outcomes of these characteristics for you as a student/child and as a teacher/adult?

In what ways have these characteristics created obstacles in your interactions, particularly as an adult?

Look at the list of teacher behaviors that encourage
obedient or responsible behavior.

As a student, which characteristics did you encounter or
observe most frequently in your teachers or other adults in
your life?

What was the impact of these behaviors on your own
attitudes, behavior, motivation, and self-concept as a
student/child and teacher/adult?

Which characteristics best describe your own teaching
behaviors and attitudes?

Choose any three characteristics you want to adopt or
improve. What are they?

Why have you chosen those characteristics?

# 4 The teacher-student relationship

p until the moment we face our first class, the bulk of our attention is focused on what and how we are going to teach. Chances are, we have learned the how-to's of explaining fractions, introducing new reading vocabulary, or demonstrating condensation. We have learned to prepare dittos, assemble a unit test, create manipulatives, and decorate bulletin boards.

With all this concentration on content, it is easy to become consumed with thoughts of *getting through the books*. It is understandable when new teachers get nervous if students are not in reading groups by the second week of school or if the other third grade teacher gets a few pages ahead in math. In departmentalized and secondary classes, limited contact with large numbers of students adds to the pressure. Curriculum guides loom overwhelmingly, and of course there are always the pressing expectations of principals, parents, and the students themselves.

Content-related pressures, whether real or self-imposed, exist in every teaching situation and with the most ideal students. And, in nearly every class, many students lack at least some of the learning, social, and self-management skills necessary to succeed in school. The pressure to cover content can become unbearable.

The whole point of discipline, or *managing* students, is to create a climate in which teaching and learning of content occur. This goal—teacher-student cooperation—is at the heart of 21st century discipline.

**Strategies are either enhanced or hampered by the nature of the relationship we establish with students.**

As teachers, we adopt specific language and behaviors to elicit positive behavior where none exists, to reinforce and maintain cooperation as it occurs, and to intervene in disruptive situations. However, the strategies we select are either enhanced or hampered by the context in which they are used: the nature and quality of the relationship we establish with our students.

The traditional emphasis on content and control in the role of the teacher formerly may have made it difficult to see what *relationships* have to do with education. Yet the teacher-student relationship forms the basis of the classroom climate in which learning can occur. The positive climate creates an instructional environment that encourages risk-taking, initiative, and personal commitment to learning.

The success of our instructional interactions with our students depends, to a large degree, on the relationship and climate we develop. Working toward a positive classroom climate—even if temporarily at the expense of the content—can help us avoid being sabotaged by negative attitudes, weak learning behaviors, and unrealistic self-expectations.

Finally, because teaching is an interactive experience, a positive teacher-student relationship increases the likelihood that the interactions will be more effective and enjoyable for all concerned.

Describe the characteristics of an ideal teacher-student relationship. **Reflection**

How can these characteristics contribute to a positive classroom climate?

How can these characteristics contribute to the students' growth and learning?
How can they encourage responsible, internally motivated cooperation (as opposed to externally motivated obedience)?

How will establishing a positive classroom climate help you achieve the goals you identified as important in the survey in Chapter 1?
If you are currently teaching, what are you doing to build a positive classroom climate?

# 5    **Needs and interactions**

I t is late Friday morning, the only time the projector was free all week. You are setting up a film that introduces material your students will need for a follow-up assignment as well as most of next week's lessons and activities. The film has to go out to another school at the end of the day.

In the meantime, it's the first nice day in nearly three weeks. There is a school festival this weekend and the anticipation has captured the attention and enthusiasm of the entire class. Not surprisingly, you are having a hard time getting the students to settle down for the movie.

This story illustrates a frequent occurrence in any group: needs in conflict. You need to show this film. The content is important and presents resources you otherwise do not have access to. You also need to avoid, if at all possible, having to restructure the majority of next week's well-sequenced plans.

At the same time, your students need some time to play, plan, run, and interact.

Both you and the kids think your own needs are important. Although they normally enjoy seeing movies, they can not see why this one is such a big deal. And even though you might understand their distractions, showing this film is a high priority for you.

You have several ways of reacting to this situation; your response is *certainly* related to your needs, particularly in the context of the relationship you have established with this group.

All behavior is motivated by needs. When facing different options, our choice is determined—consciously or not—by the strongest need. For example, perhaps later that same day you have a chance to stay after school to finish your lesson plans for next week. Doing so will satisfy a number of needs: your weekend will be free for other things; you will not have to drag home all your planning materials; and, your principal did ask you to turn in your plans, if at all possible, by the end of the day. These needs are important.

**Needs in conflict are resolved by one of three approaches: power, permissive, or cooperative**

But suppose you wish to leave immediately to meet some friends and unwind after a terribly long week. You then choose to fulfill those needs instead, take all your stuff home, set aside some planning time during the weekend, and promise your principal a copy of your plans first thing Monday morning.

The above needs illustrate personal needs in conflict. It is one thing to resolve these, but what happens when your needs clash with someone else's?

Generally, needs in conflict are resolved by one of three approaches: power (my needs overshadow yours); permissive (your needs overshadow mine); or cooperative (both sets of needs are considered and, whenever possible, both are met).

Let's go back to the movie problem. If your relationship with your students is power-oriented, you might not think about their needs: You are the teacher, they are there to work. If you use a power approach, you tell everyone to sit down and watch the film. You might use a threat to get them to do so: *Everybody settle down now. We are watching this film today. One more word about that festival and you can write about it during recess.*

If your approach is permissive, you probably give up your plans; but are likely to resent the students' lack of appreciation for your effort in getting that film. You may also become increasingly angry at the difficulties this change will present in your planning and instruction.

If you have established a cooperative atmosphere, you assert your need to show the film; describe the payoff for their patience and cooperation; and offer an early recess or perhaps some time for quiet talk as soon as they have their work finished. You might consider requiring a portion of the follow-up assignment instead of the whole thing (offering the rest for homework or even holding it until Monday). You set limits by announcing that you will run the projector as long as you have their attention. (Incidentally, this approach, although clearly the more positive of the three, will only motivate cooperation if the outcome—in this case, the extra time to interact with one another—is more meaningful and need-fulfilling than avoiding the movie. Meaningful motivators will be discussed in greater detail in Chapters 12 and 13.)

We may use different approaches for different situations, settings, and students. Each approach has pluses and minuses, as well as predictable outcomes. Each varies also in its ability to reinforce responsible cooperation over obedience.

Although nearly everyone has used or experienced each approach, each of us tends to favor one predominant model in our interactions with any given individual or group. The approach we choose is the product of a number of factors, which include: values and attitudes, previous experiences with authority relationships, the behaviors of other teachers in the school, and the way we think we should respond. In examining our responses to situations in which our needs are in conflict, we may find that we are not actually using the approach we prefer or intend, or even the one we think we are using!

For clarification, let's take a second look at each approach. The charts on the following pages define the three.

# Powering Approach (Win-Lose)

**Interaction Dynamic**

Teacher Needs OVERSHADOWS Student Needs

WIN                    LOSE

**Description**
- Demanding, power-based, authoritarian, inflexible.
- Probably the most familiar model of interaction between adults and children. Very often, the teacher may hold a powering attitude and not realize it.
- Payoff to student for cooperating includes avoidance of punishment, criticism, negative involvement with teacher.
- Little or no distinction between student behavior and student worth; equates student's poor choosing with character flaw (bad choice, bad person).
- Basic belief: *Students won't do anything right unless they are forced to.*
- Teacher may practice any or all of the following interactions: yelling, controlling, manipulating, threatening, condemning, criticizing, intimidating, punishing, advising, rescuing (out of exasperation), nagging, sarcasm, force, or attack on student's behavior, attitudes, and values.
- Competitive goal structure (nearly always, some students fail).
- General focus is negative (what student has done wrong or cannot do); may offer conditional approval (as long as student does what teacher wants); pushes for perfection.
- Outcome-oriented, usually at expense of process, geared to getting immediate results.
- Teacher makes decisions; student rarely has opportunity to offer input or make decisions (besides *DO it or else*).

**Communicates to Students**
- *I'm the boss here! What I say goes!*
- *I know what's best for you.*
- *My needs are more important than yours.*
- *I do not respect what is important to you.*
- *I can get what I want because I am bigger/more powerful/ more important than you.*

• *Because I said so.*
• *Get in your seat this minute.*
• *You keep your locker like a pigsty.*
• *I told you to get to work.*
• *If you don't do what I want, I will punish (hurt, deprive) you.*

**Examples**

• The model is familiar and well-supported by tradition.
• May get you what you want (i.e., satisfy your needs)
• Most effective with students who respond to authority, have a strong need for teacher approval, or strong fear of punishment or deprivation.

**Outcomes (Advantages)**

• Reinforces obedience, teacher-dependence, need for external validation: doing what *teacher wants*.
• Generates compliance, not commitment; encourages student to focus on keeping teacher happy (or off my back).
• Seemingly positive results tend to be temporary and not self-sustaining (i.e., requires monitoring and policing to continue).
• May generate resentment or rebellion from the student; does not accommodate student's need for personal control.
• Does not teach decision-making or responsible, self-managing behavior.
• Discourages personal empowerment (actually disempowers, inhibits initiative).
• Consequences of student's choice related to teacher reaction rather than to intrinsic benefit to student.
• Teaches student to use power (bullying, hurting, deprivation) to get what he/she wants in life; does not model compromise, negotiating, cooperation, or respect for others' needs.
• Control-oriented relationships with students can be exhausting, stressful, and unfulfilling; frustration and burnout possible.

**Outcomes (Disadvantages)**

# Permissive Approach (Lose-Win)

**Interaction
Dynamic**

**Description**

- Frequently (and incorrectly) seen as the only alternative to powering; may be employed by teachers who do not perceive themselves as having power, who find the powering model distasteful, or who are afraid of alienating students by expressing limits and needs.
- Basic belief: *If they care enough, they'll do it for me.*
- Indirect communication; specific needs of teacher unclear or rarely expressed; may expect mind reading from student.
- Dishonest; teacher frequently minimizes personal needs, then later expresses criticism or disappointment for student's lack of cooperation.
- Teacher rarely takes responsibility for own needs; may offer freedoms with little structure and few limits, and expect students to monitor themselves in appreciation.
- Teacher may offer choices to test student's loyalty, ability to guess correct choice.
- Teacher may practice any or all of the following interactions: self-pity, blaming, martyrdom, manipulating, enabling, withdrawal, disengaging, appealing to student's sense of guilt, rescuing (to protect), condemning, whining, nagging, sarcasm, indirect (or implied) attack on student's behavior, attitudes, and values.
- Teacher may make decisions and not stand by them; inconsistent in limits, tolerances, rewards, consequences, and follow-through.
- Little or no distinction between student behavior and student worth; apt to take student behavior (positive or negative) personally; disappointment and hopelessness common.
- Offers conditional approval (as long as student is doing what teacher wants); praise, when offered, is given for pleasing teacher.

- *Your needs are more important than mine.*
- *My needs are important, but so what?*
- *External approval is more important than self-care.*

**Communicates to Students**

- *I'm so sick of picking up after you kids.*
- *Look at all the work I do.*
- *You guys have it so easy.*
- *Nobody appreciates me.*

**Examples**

- May get you what you want (i.e., satisfy your needs).
- MOST effective with students who respond to guilt, fear of abandonment, or need for teacher approval.

**Outcomes (Advantages)**

- Least effective means of motivating cooperation from student, although it may get results from a student who requires teacher approval, responds to guilt, or needs to please teacher.
- Reinforces obedience, teacher-dependence, need for external validation.
- Generates compliance (if anything), not commitment.
- Does not accommodate student's need for structure and consistency; can be overwhelming, even for students who have good intentions; may cause resentment and insecurity.
- Consequences of student's choices related to teacher reaction rather than to intrinsic benefit to student.
- Does not teach decision-making or responsible, self-managing behavior; disempowers through lack of structure.
- Teaches student to use victim behavior (helplessness, manipulation) to get what he or she wants in life; does not model compromise, negotiation, cooperation, or respect for others' needs.
- Apt to take student behavior (positive or negative) personally; frustration is common.
- Failure of this approach frequently results in reversion to powering approach when teacher reaches personal limit; may also lead to quick burnout and desire to leave profession.

**Outcomes (Disadvantages)**

# Cooperative Approach (Win-Win)

**Interaction Dynamic**

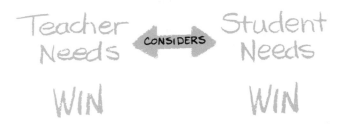

**Description**

- Teacher takes responsibility for own needs while considering needs of students.
- Characterized by direct, honest communication; teacher requests specific behavior or input.
- Teacher considers student input in final decision (or gives students specific guidelines or limits for making the decision themselves).
- Cooperative goal structure; possible for all students to succeed.
- Teacher may practice any or all of the following: offering choices within limits (expanding limits as students become better able to make decisions and self-manage); setting contingencies, supporting, listening, guiding, informing, accepting, applying natural consequences, offering recognition and reinforcement.
- Teacher focuses on the positive, building on what students can do; recognizes positive behavior by connecting cooperative choice to student benefit (positive outcome not related to teacher).
- Payoff for student cooperation: may include access to specific activities, materials, structured free time, or greater range of choices, freedoms, and responsibilities; payoff is internal and not related to reaction of teacher.
- With the cooperative approach, teacher leaves consequences of choosing (positive and negative) with students; students retain responsibility for personal choices and behavior.
- Non-life-threatening consequences to poor choices allowed as learning experience; teacher resists temptation to rescue but remains available to provide information and help students process.
- Greater consistency in teacher behavior and beliefs than in other two models.
- Process-oriented; allows students to learn from consequences of choosing.

- Teacher differentiates between student's worth and behavior and is better able to accept student as a person, even if his or her behavior is unacceptable.
- Basic belief: *Even if I can't always accommodate them, the students' needs are as valuable and important as my own.*
- Rules and limits exist in the context of the group (not the teacher's power).

- *Both our needs are important.*
- *How can we both get what we want?*
- *We can both win.*
- *You are valuable, even if you mess up.*

**Communicates to Students**

- *I will continue reading you this story as soon as it gets quiet again.*
- *I need for you to work independently so that I can finish with this group.*
- *I'm sorry you forgot your book. How are you going to do your work this period?*
- *You can choose any ten problems on this page.*
- *You can have the jump rope back as soon as you both decide how you intend to share it.*

**Examples**

- Reinforces responsible, internally motivated cooperation.
- Can accommodate students' need for control in their lives without interfering with the needs of the teacher or other students.
- Discourages resentment and rebelliousness; students recognize that their needs are heard and considered.
- Discourages teacher-dependence, victim behavior, need for external validation.
- Helps students make connection between *what I do* and *what happens to me* at an internal level.
- Consequence of student's choice related to intrinsic benefits; builds personal empowerment, enhances student's self-concept, and reinforces responsibility for personal choices and behavior.
- Generates commitment; students have a stake in the success of the classroom.

**Outcomes (Advantages)**

- Process-oriented; allows students to learn from consequences of choosing.
- Encourages student to focus on personal needs within set limits and to consider the needs of the teacher and other students.
- Results tend to be long-term, self-sustaining, and do not require constant monitoring from teacher, although reinforcement helps.
- Teaches decision-making and responsible, self-managing behavior.
- Models compromise, negotiation, cooperation, and respect for each other's needs.
- Teaches student that it is possible and desirable to get what you want in life without hurting or depriving anyone else.

**Outcomes (Disadvantages)**

- Because this method is process-oriented, it may take longer.
- Building student self-management may require teaching students specific skills and allowing them to practice.
- Less familiar than the other two models; may require learning new interaction, self-care, and self-expression skills; may require restructuring perception of authority relationships.
- May be perceived as permissive by people who favor powering model (or do not know anything else); may not receive support or acceptance from administration or other teachers (until they see the results).

Listed below and on the following page are several scenarios. For each, think through what you want the students to be doing and what your needs are; specify these as your objectives. Then think of the way you might word a powering response, a permissive response, and a cooperative response. Write the responses as quotations.

---

Jasmine's work area is a mess. You nearly tripped over her pile of papers as you walked past her chair.

Objective (what you want/your needs):

Powering response:

Permissive response:

Cooperative response:

Lamont and David want to sit together during independent work time.

Objective:

Powering response:

Permissive response:

Cooperative response:

You have assigned three worksheets but your students would prefer to work on the word search puzzle they got in another class earlier today.

Objective:

Powering response:

Permissive response:

Cooperative response:

Adrian spent the entire library period absorbed in a new adventure book. At the end of class, she pleads with you to allow her to check out the book so she can finish it at home. Adrian has not returned the books she borrowed four weeks ago.

Objective:

Powering response:

Permissive response:

Cooperative response:

Relate the activities on the next few pages to actual experi-  **Activity**
ences. If your teaching experience is limited, you can
complete this exercise by substituting the word *child, sib-
ling, co-worker, roommate, partner,* in place of the word
*student.* You will find the dynamics to be remarkably similar. If possible, try to keep the same reference group for all
three activities.

---

Can you think of a time you used the powering approach
in an interaction with a student (or group of students)?

Describe the situation:

Your needs:

Your students' needs:

Your reaction (behavior, language):

Short-term (immediate) outcome:

Long-term outcome:

What you learned:

Alternate reaction (behavior, language):

How could this alternative accommodate both sets of
needs more effectively?

Can you think of a time you used the permissive approach in an interaction with a student (or group of students).

Describe the situation:

Your needs:

Your students' needs:

Your reaction (behavior, language):

Short-term (immediate) outcome:

Long-term outcome:

What you learned:

Alternate reaction (behavior, language):

How could this alternative accommodate both sets of needs more effectively?

Can you think of a time you used the cooperative approach in an interaction with a student (or group of students)?

Describe the situation:

Your needs:

Your students' needs:

Your reaction (behavior, language):

Short-term (immediate) outcome:

Long-term outcome:

What you learned:

Alternate reaction (behavior, language):

How could this alternative accommodate both sets of needs more effectively?

# 6 The win-win classroom

I n the previous chapter, we saw that attempts to control students have two main drawbacks. First of all, whether we try to control directly, through powering, or indirectly, through manipulation, we run full tilt into a fact of human nature: people generally do not like to be controlled. Even students who seem to enjoy or require being controlled often do so to limit the responsibility they have to take for their lives (if someone else is calling the shots and can be blamed for everything, a student has to assume very little responsibility). Normally—and quite naturally—we resist other people's attempts to tell us how to act, what to wear, and so on. (What's your first reaction when you see a *Wet Paint! Do not Touch!* sign?)

Second, we see how subjecting students to our control not only uses a lot of time and energy, but also deprives them of opportunities to develop responsibility, self-confidence, self-esteem, *and* important self-management skills.

We all need to feel a sense of control of our lives. At the same time, each of us needs a certain degree of structure in order to exercise control constructively. Helping students develop responsibility and self-management skills requires that we offer them a little of both. Powering hinders the students' sense of control; permissiveness denies them adequate structure.

Fortunately, it is possible to accommodate the need for students to experience control in their lives without having them interfere with the safety and welfare of anyone else— including us! And it is likewise possible to accommodate their need for structure without preventing them from learning to think. A win-win classroom is characterized by clear and specific limits with opportunities to make choices and experience power within those limits. Everyone is offered a stake in the success of the classroom and everyone has a chance to succeed. Each student is encouraged to be responsible for his or her behavior and consequences are tied to the choices each individual makes.

In a win-win classroom, the teacher is on the same side as the students and the students know it. Individual needs and feelings are valued and, although it may frequently be impossible for everyone to win, there is usually room for flexibility, negotiation, and compromise. No one needs to win at anyone else's expense. As the cooperative climate develops, resistance and rebellion become increasingly pointless. Attention shifts from teacher-control to student self-control, and from discipline to instruction.

The notion of win-win classroom management can be disconcerting at first, especially to power-oriented teachers. Considering the tradition of an autocratic teaching role, the expectations of administrators, pressures from parents, needs of students, and demands of curriculum and content, how does this model fit?

As long as only teachers are accountable and responsible for what goes on in their classrooms, authority relationships will exist between teachers and students. Both win-win and win-lose approaches demand an element of power (authority) on the part of the teacher, because the teacher is the adult. Teachers have the power to set goals, limits, and contingencies, and, if necessary, have the final word on what works in the best interests of the group. But in the win-win classroom, the power of the teacher does not connote the force that characterized the win-lose authority relationships of previous eras. The goal of power is not to assert ourselves as controlling, punitive, threatening, or more important than

> In a win-win classroom, the teacher is on the same side as students, and they know it.

our students. Instead, power in win-win relationships translates to *empowering* students within rules and limits that likewise accommodate the needs of the teacher: *We function within a certain set of rules, not because I'm bigger, not because I'll like you more, but because we all benefit when these rules are followed.*

Unfortunately, the models of interaction familiar to most of us simply cannot strike that balance; we need an entirely new way of working with students to achieve that middle ground. Yet, even with a firm commitment to win-win, it is annoyingly easy to revert back to the other models without thinking. As with any behavior change, we need a new set of behaviors, the willingness to make a conscious effort, and the patience and faith to practice what we want to set in motion.

The rest of this book looks at the specific behaviors necessary for positively reconstructing authority relationships that encourage student self-control and reduce the need for teacher involvement in classroom management and discipline. The next section addresses specific teacher behaviors that we can choose to make it more likely for each of our students to succeed. This success orientation is crucial to the effectiveness of the *win-win* alternative.

# Section Two

# Success Orientation

# 7    Expectations and routines

Most of us enter the teaching profession with all sorts of expectations—conscious and subconscious. Based on what we hope for from our students, what we hear from other teachers, and what we believe we can and will do, we construct a picture of a classroom that may or may not reflect the reality we encounter.

In addition, perhaps we have also heard that high expectations generate high performance. True, we will not get much out of kids we do not ultimately believe in, but too often, *high expectations* is a synonym for wishful thinking. For example, early in my teaching career, I presented my students with my idea of a perfect lesson. I had orchestrated an environment based on elaborate plans, plenty of materials, color-coded direction cards, and enough stimulating activities to keep them all busy until Thanksgiving. These kids were in fifth grade, some of them for the third time; certainly they would be able to navigate the work centers under my watchful, nurturing, facilitating care. Right?

Wrong. For starters, no one at the mural center could agree on a theme; the kids in the media corner were screaming and fighting over who would operate the projector; and all the markers for the art activity mysteriously vanished within the first ten seconds of class. Evidently no one had ever worked with a ruler or used an encyclopedia before, and, although I had explained everything inside and out, I had a steady stream of kids tugging on my sleeve asking me what they were supposed to do. I stood in amazement, watching weeks of planning and work end in chaos. In the midst of it, all I could think was: *But I laminated everything!*

I received two shocks that day. First, I had expected my creativity to carry more weight than it actually did; instead, it was unappreciated and overwhelming. Second, I had expected the students, who seemed mature and streetwise, to have already acquired certain responsible learning behaviors. Yet they were unable to work independently in small groups, care for materials, or make decisions about their learning. It seemed as though my expectations were actually creating problems.

Now what?

During this time, my students were visiting Mr. Grey for art twice a week. When they came back from his class, I would ask them what they had done. Each report detailed monotonous exercises such as getting the scissors out of a box, putting the lid back on the box, putting the box back in the cabinet, sitting down with the scissors, then putting the scissors back again, and so on. Over and over. For the first few days of school, the kids did nothing besides practice getting, holding, passing, using, and returning the things they needed for art.

I asked Mr. Grey what he was up to. *Don't you have a curriculum to get through this year?*

*I sure do, and it's massive. But if we don't do this first, we'll never get through any of it.*

*You mean to tell me that these kids don't know how to get paint jars out of a storage closet?*

*Some do, sure. But most don't. Or at least they don't think about it on their own. This way, there are no questions later about where things go or how I expect them to be used.*

There was that word again. *Don't you EXPECT them to know this stuff?*

*It doesn't matter. I still have to show them. Then, maybe, I have a right to my expectations.*

It was true. No one had higher expectations for the students than Mr. Grey. But no one gave the kids more training

**Each report detailed monotonous exercises such as, getting the scissors out, putting the lid on the box, putting the box back, and so on. Over and over.**

for success, either.

It is disappointing to discover that entering an inspiring classroom environment does not trigger some magic hormone that enables children to use a pencil sharpener, recap the paste, alphabetize resource books, or move around the room nondisruptively. Simply expecting certain behaviors does not guarantee they will occur even if the lessons are well-planned, and your mood is positive and enthusiastic. (Besides, if students cooperate only because we expect or want their cooperation, we are back to eliciting obedient, teacher-pleasing behavior.) Without information, instruction, and guided practice, we actually doom our students— and ourselves—to failure. Clearly, there is more to generating cooperation than simply expecting and modeling it.

To make the best use of our expectations, we have to consider three steps. The first is knowing what is needed; think about the behaviors and skills your students will use to complete a particular task or function independently and responsibly in your class. There are hidden assumptions and expectations in every lesson we plan. *Don't take anything for granted!* Do they need to know how to handle science equipment? Use a dictionary? Work with a partner? Move to various parts of the room? Follow written directions? Staple papers together? Put their assignments in a particular place?

You must also know what YOU want. Do you require a certain heading on the papers they turn in? Do you want them to push in their chairs before they leave the room? Will it drive you crazy if someone starts to sharpen a pencil while you are addressing the whole group? Where do you want the counters kept when the students are finished with them?

Numerous problems and conflicts can be avoided by simply expressing what you want, especially if it is mentioned *before* the kids have a chance to mess up. Talk about these personal classroom requirements with your students. Encourage them to share theirs.

Obviously you cannot predict every single need that will arise, but the better you can account for the skills and behaviors your activities demand, the better you can plan for success. Also, the more clear and specific you are in identifying these needs, the less likely you are to be undermined by students' confusion, frustration, or ineptness.

Next, identify the levels of ability and responsibility your students have. Watch them work—or not work. What happens when you ask them to do something? Can they solve problems on their own or ask a classmate for assistance without disrupting others when you need a few uninterrupted minutes? Are

**Problems and conflicts can be avoided by simply expressing what you want, *before* kids have a chance to mess up.**

they bewildered by choices or directions? What do your shelves look like at the end of the day?

Assume nothing other than the fact that your students may not be sure what you want. In fact, it may be most effective to assume the worst—which is not the same as expecting the worst—and start from there. Sure, they probably know how to take care of the books in the classroom library, but they may not know how you want them to do it.

**Start where they are and build success on success.**

Finally, set aside some time to fill the gap between what you need and what they can do. Start where they are and build success on success. I once had a group of high-risk eighth graders spend a few minutes practicing putting the caps on markers. They enjoyed writing with them, yet I could not afford to keep replacing them when the markers dried out. I did a half-humorous lesson on recapping the pens, making sure that we listened for the click that indicated they were on tight (most of the kids did not know that trick). Not only did the markers seem to last forever, but the students became remarkably committed to their care.

Don't hesitate to have your kids walk through daily routines. Take a few minutes here and there to have them practice moving from their work area to the reading group before you start teaching reading in groups. Have one small group at a time learn to run the listening post before they use it in a center.

Unless you intend to spend your entire year guarding, dispensing, and retrieving classroom materials, teach your students how to get, use, and return things when they are finished. Put various kids in charge to help you monitor the care of materials. I once decided the best person to keep track of the cards in our handwriting program was the third grader who seemed to lose track of them most often. She took her job quite seriously: Not only did she never lose a card from that point on, but she once kept the entire class from going to lunch until the capital R card turned up!

The points mentioned above are especially true if you are working with younger children or students who always seem to need your help and attention. Have the entire group practice working independently. At times, put yourself off limits while you work at your desk. Start with a one- or two-minute interval if necessary and refuse all contact during that time.

But make sure students have something to keep them busy, something they can do easily at first, such as review work, practice drills, or a puzzle. Remember, your goal here is to reinforce independence—not teach content. Encourage students to help one another or go on to a different task until you are available to help. Gradually increase the amount of time and the complexity of the tasks. As their skills build, you will become increasingly comfortable working with small groups and assigning tasks that require independent work habits.

Instruction, guidelines, and practice make responsibility and self-management a reality. Combined with meaningful consequences for cooperation and opportunities to succeed, this type of preparation contributes to the positive behaviors that high expectations can inspire.

**Activity**    It is easy to get tripped up by assumptions and expectations. Look at the lessons you have planned for the next day or two. In each, determine all the skills and behaviors that your students will need in order to successfully complete the activities you have planned, such as: use a ruler to measure, retrieve materials from a particular place, construct an outline, choose a sequence, and so on.

Which skills/behaviors have you observed your students successfully performing?

Which of these skills/behaviors have you presented or demonstrated?

Which have your students practiced?

In what way have you addressed the need for these skills/behaviors in your planning?

There are certain behaviors that bother each of us: people who play with their loose change, rock back on their chairs, interrupt others, or walk around with their shoelaces untied. What are yours?

Go back and mark (check, circle, highlight) the items in the above examples that occur in your classroom. What have you done to try to prevent these actions from happening? What else might you do?

# 8    Consistency

Well-meaning experts often caution new teachers to be consistent without ever talking about what that term implies. Consistency is a very important component of the structure we provide; its absence provokes student insecurity at best, distrust and chaos at worst. It permeates all levels of teacher behavior, personal and interactive, and involves language, values, expectations, feelings, and needs.

Perhaps at the simplest level, we need consistency from one day to the next in our expectations, tolerances, and limits. For example, if our students are accustomed to an acceptable noise level during work time every day, it is not fair to yell at them when the same noise level gets on our nerves on one particular day. True, our limits vary from time to time: a run-in with a neighbor, congested traffic on the way to work, or finding out the rent check bounced may make us feel irritated by things that ordinarily would not bother us. Realizing this, we should warn the kids ahead of time that, at least for today, the rules have changed.

Different situations test consistency. Obviously, we allow different behaviors on a playground than in a library, and special events like field trips or guest speakers require different rules than normal classroom activities. But we should not suddenly lash out at previously accepted behavior just because the principal is in the room. When different activities, situations, or circumstances require a departure from the normal structure, we must adequately prepare our students by letting them know beforehand the new limits that apply.

What about consistency between our behavior and that of the other teachers in the school—particularly other teachers our kids see? We can count on our students to confront us about any inconsistencies that do not work in their behalf: *But Mr. Peterson never gives homework!* The rules and privileges extended by different teachers reflect differences in personalities, tolerances, and needs. These differences are not inconsistencies; we do not control other people's behaviors. Trying to model their behavior for the sake of consistency is silly and self-defeating. If we don't need absolute silence in our room, why demand it because the other social studies teachers do? If our kids get their seatwork done while listening to music, prefer to work with a partner, or chew gum, and these behaviors are acceptable to us, applying someone else's standards will only meet that person's needs—not ours.

Sure, setting standards and limits that apply to personal needs may require that our students shift gears when they go from one class to another because it is likely that our needs will demand a slightly different set of rules than some other teacher's. But our students will certainly encounter a variety of people throughout their school careers (and lives); let's allow them to develop the flexibility they will need to relate to these different personalities. [1]

Another dimension of consistency involves role modeling. How similar is our behavior to what we expect of our students? Turn back to the survey in Chapter 1 and look at the behaviors you identified as highly desirable for your students. How high do you score on the same items? What about other behaviors? Are we on time as frequently as we expect the students to be? When we mess up, do we take responsibility for our mistakes, catch ourselves before we make excuses or cast blame? Are our desk, handwriting, and appearance neat?

Even more important, how do we talk to students? Would we accept the same language and tone from them? How would we feel if someone we cared about talked to us the way we talk to our students? (If we speak in a way that arouses fear, anger, resentment, or embarrassment in us, we can be sure our students react in the same way.) Would we talk to adults the way we talk to our students? Kids can see through a double standard. On the other hand, a high degree of consistency between what is acceptable for us and what is acceptable for them builds success and win-win.

What about the consistency between what we say and what we do? One first-year teacher asked me to observe how consistently she was recognizing only students who raise their hands. She started by announcing, *We need to take turns in this discussion. From this point on, I'll call on you only if you raise your hand first.*

One student reacted, of course, without raising his hand: *Really?*

*Yes, I mean it,* she answered, undermining her own admonition.

Is the comment *I'll only say this once.* an introduction to something we repeat all afternoon? Do we spend a lot of time warning, reminding, and nagging? Do we interact with students who are at our side seconds after asking them to stay in their seats? These inconsistencies erode our credibility with students. (I knew I was in trouble once when a student responded to my frustration by indignantly claiming, *You only told me once!*) Breaking out of these self-defeating traps requires awareness and practice. Outside observation and feedback, or personally keeping count of instances in which you do behave consistently, can be helpful.

Other areas of consistency are more tricky and subtle. They involve the relationships between feelings, values, and language, and are crucial to the quality of classroom climate and our relationships with students.

First, let us look at the consistency between our feelings and words. Accurately expressing feelings can be challenging, particularly in high-stress situations. Have you ever had a child rock a little too far back in her seat and then come crashing down on the floor? What did you feel at that moment? You were probably startled by the noise and frightened for the child's safety. How did you react? If you are good at this, you might have asked if the child was all right and then said, *Wow! That really startled me! I was afraid you were hurt!*

But is that how most of us react? Our fear and frustration (How many times have I told this kid not to rock back in her seat?) probably came out: *Don't you even know how to sit on a*

**Is the comment, *I'll only say this once!* an introduction to something repeated all afternoon?**

*chair?*

The danger in this type of inconsistency is that the child tends to hear only the emotion in the words and misinterprets the feelings expressed. It is highly unlikely that this student will be thinking, *Gee, my teacher must really have been startled. She's only yelling at me because she's having difficulty dealing with her fear for my safety.* What she hears is simply another vote for her clumsiness and inadequacy.

To recognize and modify inconsistencies between our feelings and language is a challenge and demands that we learn to: wait a few seconds to respond—instead of react to emotional or high-stress situations; think about what we feel before the words come out of our mouths; and learn to express our anger, fear, and frustration without personally attacking the child (more on this in later chapters).

Along these lines, we also should keep an eye out for consistency between what we want and what we say. For example, if seeing blocks scattered over the rug upsets us, there are different ways we might react. One is an attack: *You are so thoughtless and inconsiderate! Get over here and pick up these blocks this instant!* Another is to ask students to *Please pick up the blocks for me.* This may get the same results, but for an entirely different reason—teacher-pleasing. A third response is to request students to *Please pick up the blocks so that no one trips over them.*, and conveys meaningful consequences quite clearly. If all we want is to get those blocks off the floor, then it probably doesn't matter which approach we use. But if we not only want to get the blocks put away but also want to reinforce self-management and intrinsic consequences, then we certainly want to try to avoid the first two examples.

**The words and actions we choose will either help us or create obstacles.**

Many of the problems in consistency, such as those mentioned above, may be the natural result of a larger, deeper gap between information-age values (such as independence, initiative, decision-making, and self-management) and industrial-age behaviors (powering, punishing, and offering few options). Bridging this gap begins with an awareness of and commitment to win-win outcomes. With this awareness, we can begin to check the behaviors and language we are tempted to choose. For example, we can examine our behaviors and ask if our particular feedback reinforces independence; if the provided structure encourages self-management; and if the response to a student's comments or actions promotes empowerment and self-esteem.

The words and actions we choose will either help us reach our goals or create obstacles. Consistency requires each of us, as adults working with children, to become aware of and responsible for our language and behaviors. Each time we try it gets easier *and* brings us closer to the positive, cooperative climate of a 21st century classroom.

---

[1] See Question #6, page 83, in the Activity at the end of this chapter.

**Activity**   1. On a sheet of paper, list two columns. In the first, list five or more behaviors you want your students to demonstrate. In column two, evaluate your own consistency on the same behaviors on a scale of 1 (rarely) to 5 (almost always). For example, if you have listed *be on time*, you might answer 1 (rarely). If you list *come prepared*, you might respond 3 (half of the time).

2. Now, describe an instance in which you were challenged to maintain consistency between what you expect of your students and your own behavior.

   a. How was that situation resolved?

   b. What are you doing to maintain consistency at this level?

3. Describe an instance in which you were challenged to maintain consistency from one day to the next.

   a. How was that situation resolved?

   b. What are you doing to maintain consistency at this level?

4. Describe an instance in which you were challenged to maintain consistency between your feelings and your language (words, tone, facial expressions).

   a. How was that situation resolved?

   b. What are you doing to maintain consistency at this level?

5. Describe an instance in which you were challenged to maintain consistency between your language (requests, directions, feedback) and your objectives (student responsibility, initiative, internal motivation, or self-management).

   a. How was that situation resolved?

   b. What are you doing to maintain consistency at this level?

6. If your students seem to have a hard time with differences in the needs, rules, limits, or tolerances from one teacher to the next, involve them in discussions about similarities and differences among their teachers, and, perhaps, among siblings and friends. Possible discussion starters include:

   a. Tell me something you like about each one of your teachers.

   b. What are you allowed to do at home that you cannot do in school?

   c. In what ways are your friends alike? How do they differ?

# 9    **Focus and feedback**

**A** major portion of interactions with students involves giving them feedback and information on their performances in our class-rooms. The type and quality of feedback offered reflects our focus and perceptions. Choosing a success-oriented focus can have an excep-tionally positive impact on these interactions.

We have a tremendous amount of control over the way we look at any given person, action, or thing. For example, as you are reading this, you are probably sitting or lying on some piece of furniture. Take a good look at whatever piece of furniture you have selected. Let's assume your body is being supported by a chair.

Find five things wrong with the chair. Maybe it is too hard. An ugly, dull color. Too heavy. Too far from the window. In a draft. (If you are in a really miserable mood, you can probably go on for an hour.)

OK. Now that we know what is wrong with the chair, let's try something else. It may help if you leave the room for a while and then return. If not, shut your eyes for a few seconds before you try the following.

Now, look at this wonderful chair and state at least five great things about it! It gives fantastic support. It is a wonderfully neutral color. It is sturdy. In a cozy corner. In a well-ventilated space. And so on.

Did the chair change? Probably not, in the few seconds between these exercises. The only thing that changed is the way you looked at the chair and what you focused on. (You may have even noticed a slight change in your breathing, your comfort, and your mood.) Consider how powerful a positive perspective can be! This is the case with students, too. In any given incident, interaction, or assignment, we can find something wrong. But any time we can find something to criticize, we can likewise find something positive.

To illustrate, a teacher received a paper from one of her second-grade students. The drawing on the paper was little more than an angry black scribble. Instead of a story, there was a sentence fragment without a capital, no punctuation, and not one correctly spelled word. Attempts to erase stray pencil marks had left several holes and the paper had been crumpled at least once in frustration.

The other students had all received stickers with some positive comments about their work. But this paper was something else! Naturally, the teacher's first instinct was to take out a red pencil and correct the paper. Her only hesitation was not knowing where to start, but this gave her a few seconds to think. Here was a product that had *I can't* written all over it: What would her criticisms contribute?

So she made a note to work with this student on capital letters and spelling, and to remember to show him how to use an eraser without mauling the paper. And, as she had done for the other students, she placed a sticker on the top. Finding something positive was a challenge, although shifting back to that goal enabled her to see the one thing the student had not messed up. She returned his paper marked *Magnificent Margins!*

What did this teacher communicate to the student? At no point was she saying that fragments instead of sentences were OK or that crumpling the paper was acceptable. But instead of seeing them as the student's failure, she chose to see them as something he simply had not learned to do yet. Her primary goal was to encourage this child to continue learning; she started with what he had done right and developed a plan to teach him the rest.

Of course the student was delighted with his sticker. The

**She chose to see them as something he simply had not yet learned to do.**

positive focus helped him to begin to turn his *I can't* perceptions into *I can*. Building on the pride of his magnificent margins, with further instruction, positive feedback on what he was doing right, and a little time, his work improved steadily. He was increasingly willing to take risks and try new things. The shift in the teacher's focus broke the *failure loop* that had strengthened his *I can't* beliefs.

A success-oriented focus means that the time we take to evaluate our students' work has a greater purpose than simply coming up with numbers to put in the little boxes in our grade books. In most situations, evaluations boil down to some letter, number, or mark, which represents an opinion of someone else's achievement, effort, or behavior. In the school setting, these opinions are called grades. We sometimes use them to motivate students, although many teachers claim that students have become increasingly resistant over the past few decades to this form of motivation. (Grades are, however, still effective with high-achieving students who see high marks as meaningful and accessible. Grades will rarely motivate students with a history of low scores and negative self-perceptions; nor will they inspire students who simply do not care about grades—regardless of potential or past achievement.)

In general, our grading practices focus on mistakes and deficiencies; most often, the marks on a paper comment on what the student did incorrectly. Consider the students who hand in something done completely wrong. In the win-lose classroom, the teacher probably gives the student a zero and rationalizes, *I already explained this twice.* or *Well, she should have been listening.* In the win-win classroom, the student can get credit for her efforts, remedial work to correct her misunderstanding, and another chance to do it right.

In win-lose classrooms, poor grades are sometimes used as a powering technique to punish uncooperative students. A poor grade can discourage a gifted, *can-do* student; for a typically low-achieving student, poor grades simply reinforce the *can't-do* attitude that accompanies low self-esteem. (A number of teachers suggest switching from a red marker to another color—blue, black, or green—to make comments and corrections seem less critical or punitive.)

As a solitary form of feedback, grades are extremely limiting. Unless our criteria for grading each assignment are sharply focused and well-communicated, the grades we give tell our students very little about what students can do. A grade of *B−* on a writing assignment says little more than *This is not as good as the one that got the B+.* This grade

> **In the win-win classroom, the student can get credit for efforts, remedial work, and another chance to do the assignment right.**

certainly does not tell the student which concepts he misunderstood or where he needs additional work. A grade of 76 percent tells the student she understood 76 percent of the content on the assignment or that she can do a particular skill 76 percent of the time. What does this mean in terms of learning needs?

For the majority of teachers, grades are a fact of life—like them or not—and a tradition that is accepted and understood by parents and administrators. Grades work for us because they are easier to record and communicate than descriptive evaluations. But if we have to live with grades, then let them work for the students as well, by keeping our focus on what the student is doing right and highlighting areas that need improvement, and by using grades to tell us what we need to teach and reinforce.

One of my fourth-graders, who made a career out of testing me, wrote a long, wonderful story for a writing assignment. One of the criteria for this task was that the final product be presented in cursive handwriting. Although the rule was an old standby, this student handed in three pages in his neatest printing; everything else was fine.

I was at a crossroads—do I give him a lower grade because he printed and disregard all the writing he had done? Do I ignore the printing? Not comfortable with either option, I read the story, which was excellent, and told him it was a great first draft; I would be happy to accept it when it was completed. He had a choice at that point: lose points for printing but get credit for a great story or rewrite the story for full credit. He had choices within limits; either option was OK with me. I made it clear that I appreciated and enjoyed the work he did and still valued him regardless of his choice.

Offering students the chance to renegotiate a grade puts a great deal of responsibility on the student, requiring more time and effort for him or her to devote to learning, correcting, and redoing. This choice leaves the door open for greater success (in terms of better grades and advancement to new content) while also allowing the student to accept the grade for the effort he or she has made. In this way, grades are simply a reflection of how the student is doing on this particular project so far, and feedback the student can use in making decisions about personal learning goals.

A positive focus need not be solely reflected in our evaluations of our students' work. A high-school teacher made it a point each day to individually greet as many of his 150 students as possible. He met quite a few at the door as they were coming in and greeted the rest while walking around during their independent work time. His comments may not have been terribly elaborate, ranging from a simple *Hi* or *How was your weekend?* to *I really enjoyed reading your essay last night.* or just *Glad you're here.*

Yet he found that looking for something positive to say to his students helped to improve the overall classroom climate, his relationships with students, and his attitude. He was able to notice positive qualities in the most difficult students. He learned to appreciate something in each student and communicated his appreciation for the special contribution each one made. He still required students to operate within the limits set for the classroom, corrected errors in work, and intervened in disruptions. But each student felt valued and accepted at the same time.

A positive focus can also help us avoid unnecessary conflicts and confrontations. One day I was detained for a minute on my way back from lunch and returned to thirty-nine loud and disorderly students. They were so wound up they barely noticed me and certainly did not hear my request to settle down and sit at their desks until I finally blew up and yelled at them to sit and put their heads down!

They were quite surprised; this was not my usual way of dealing with this normally cooperative and—by this point in the year—self-managing class. Just as I was beginning to calm down, I noticed that one of the kids still had not gotten back. At that moment, she ambled into the class, looked at her classmates with their heads on their arms, and before I had a chance to jump all over her, said, *What are we playing?*

I was on the edge: had I not burst out laughing, I might have later been indicted for murdering an entire fifth grade class. To this day, I'm not convinced that the decision to laugh was entirely conscious, but it certainly defused the tension. We were able to move on to a more important matter—instruction—with the normally safe and positive climate restored.

Focus also refers to our ability to separate students from their behavior. This task is probably the most difficult aspect of orienting our perceptions to success. When a student (or anyone) does something we find particularly annoying, it is difficult to see beyond the offending behavior. We forget the nice smile, the great strides in math, the interest in turtles: the person is reduced to *someone-who-does-not-remember-library-books.*

Now this is not to suggest that we take time out while little Joey is torturing the Jade plant to make a mental list of his great qualities. Our focus does not keep us from intervening

**To separate students from their behavior is probably the most difficult aspect of orienting our perceptions to success.**

during negative behaviors; it simply enables us to remember that Joey is more than the particular behavior he is distastefully exhibiting at the moment.

Being able to separate the child from his or her behavior has important consequences for our behavior and our relationships with the child. To begin, we are better able to resolve the problem without attacking the child personally. The behavior may be wrong, but Joey—his self-worth, the essence of who he is—is not. We are better able, then, to accept the student, even though we do not accept the behavior. We are able to impose the necessary consequence and still value the person.

There are many times when we find ourselves looking at the hole more often than we notice the doughnut—when we find our comments more negative than positive. This is understandable. Criticism and negativity sometimes occurred in the warmest adult-child relationships in the industrial era. As society changes, however, the needs of society also change, which is why many of the old ways which characterized the factory economy cannot work in today's information age. [1]

**Proclaim a positive period.** Because the patterns may be painfully familiar, a conscious shift toward a more positive focus may pose a real challenge. There are a number of things you can do to help maintain a positive attitude, from creating a pleasing and comfortable physical environment in your classroom to consciously changing language and behavior. Commit to noticing a student you have not spent much time with lately. Proclaim a positive period in which your written comments on student papers give feedback only on what they have done correctly. (You may want to extend this positive period indefinitely.) Make a point to recognize something positive in another teacher—and let that person know it. Promise yourself not to complain or make one negative comment about a student, teacher, parent, administrator, or administrative policy during your lunch break, in the teachers' lounge, or during a faculty meeting. And in turn, ask your students for feedback on what you are doing well!

One middle-school teacher claimed to have been helped by putting little plus signs around her room and at home (on her mirror, in her purse, on her car's dashboard). The cards were reminders that she had a choice, but she found the cards started building more positive outlooks in her students and family as well.

Every interaction and event in our lives gives us an opportunity to choose how we are going to respond. Sure, it may be more automatic to blow up, worry, or complain, but these reactions cost us—socially, physically, and emotionally. In the most stressful situations, we have a choice about our own behavior and outlook. (Sometimes pausing for a few seconds can help, not only to avoid doing or saying something that might be hurtful or alienating, but also to remind us that we have other options.) The more frequently we remember to take the more positive route, the greater the benefits. We can build trust and avoid conflict in our interactions with others, reduce stress levels and symptoms, and increase the amount of satisfaction and contentment in our lives.

---

[1] That is also why it is often so difficult to switch to new behaviors, particularly within the context of an institution that operates with a generally negative orientation of a power-based win-lose model. For more information read Alice Miller, *For Your Own Good: Hidden Cruelty in Child-Rearing and the Roots of Violence*. Farrar, Straus, and Giroux, New York. 1983.

**Activity**   On a separate paper, draw a chart with two columns such as the one below. In column one, describe several occasions that evoked or tempted a negative response from you. In column two, write down a more positive response you could have used instead. After this exercise, focus on the following questions.

| Occasion | Positive response |
|----------|-------------------|
|          |                   |

In what ways is your verbal feedback to students positively focused and success-oriented?

In what ways is your written feedback to students (grades, items checked on papers, comments on written assignments, essays, tests, and so on) positively focused and success-oriented?

What sort of information do you collect and record to keep track of student progress and performance (letter grades, percentages, anecdotal records or other descriptive data, skill checklists, and so on)?

In what ways does your evaluation of student progress and performance influence teaching decisions (pacing, materials, review, assignments, and so forth) for individual students in your class?

What opportunities do your students have to change, improve, or renegotiate grades?

What have you done to maintain a positive focus in the classroom?

What have you done to encourage your students to maintain a positive focus about themselves, school, their friends, their work, and other aspects of their lives?

# 10 Giving instructions

I was once observing a student teacher during the first week of school, who announced to her kindergarten class that it was time to get in line. A few students stopped and stared; the others started running around the room. It was chaotic. I wondered if *Get in line!* was some strange new game, until one five-year-old came up and asked the teacher, *What's a line?*

We know that our students need clear instructions to succeed at the tasks set before them, but what could be more clear than *Get in line*? As that student teacher quickly found out, instructions are clear only if the students understand them. The statement *Get in line!* assumes they know what a line is, where it starts and ends, which way to face, whether it is single- or double-file, and all other rules regarding talking, touching, and what, if anything, the students should carry with them. She may as well have given the directions in another language. Imagine the confusion possible with more complex assignments!

The goal of success-oriented instructions goes beyond simply getting the students to do what they need to do. We have a number of choices about the way we give instructions to our students. Depending upon the choices we make, we set the students up for failure and confusion or help them build responsibility and self-esteem.

Lack of clarity, as in the previous example, is a common problem in giving directions. For the student, not knowing what to do becomes a source of confusion, helplessness, and feelings of inadequacy. Poorly communicated instructions also build teacher-dependence, waste time, and often result in negative feedback. We can avoid these pitfalls by breaking down the directions step by step, especially the first time we ask students to do something. Walk the students through each step of the directions, particularly those involved with routines, the use of equipment, materials, or movement. This will increase the likelihood of success. Remember, if it is important to us, it's worth the time.

To aid in clarifying directions, be careful about the adjectives used. We know what we mean by *good* handwriting, *exciting* characters, *thorough* research, and *clear* presentation. Do they? Do we let them know before their work ends up on our desks how we will evaluate a project for particular skills? Telling them what we are looking for or grading for helps focus students' efforts and promotes success.

Students are bombarded with verbal instructions from teachers and other adults, as well as written instructions from books, the blackboard, and assignments. Simple directions, given one at a time, can probably get through to just about any student who is listening. Once students know specifically what you mean by *Clear off your desks!*, you probably will not need to clarify it further or put it in writing. However, in new or more involved situations, students can benefit by directions provided in as many ways as possible.

For example, announcing that a group is to do the first ten problems on page 86 and any five problems on page 93 might be fine for auditory learners (who are really listening), but other students may need additional cues. Writing the directions on the board, in a folder, or on a task card can serve as a reminder and learning aid for these students. Written instructions also free us to move on to other tasks. Once we have given our instructions in oral and written form, the students have recourse to something besides bothering Teacher with questions about *what page?* or *which problems?* Following written directions helps develop independence, especially in poor readers or very young students.

Success-oriented instructions are also well-sequenced. In one episode of a popular TV series the characters attempted to defuse a bomb according to step-by-step directions read to them. *Unscrew the wing nut on the end.* They do. *Remove the tail assembly.* They do. *Cut the wires leading to the timing device.* They do. *But first . . .*

The result of unclear sequencing of classroom directions may not be quite as harrowing, but it does present additional opportunities to make mistakes. Listing the steps in specific order is essential, particularly with projects that involve a number of steps; writing and numbering the directions helps a great deal.

**Ask for their attention and WAIT—until desks are cleared and students are looking at you.**

We can also make success-oriented decisions about when to give instructions. Have you ever gotten your kids busy on some task, then suddenly remembered a point you forgot to mention while they were still listening? Did you ask them to stop working so that you could mention the particular point? If we give information to students without first asking for their attention and better still—eye contact, we should not be too surprised when the majority get it wrong.

Ask for their attention and wait, WAIT, until they get their desks cleared and are looking at you. Giving directions to inattentive students communicates a lack of self-respect (you are worth listening to, aren't you?) and sets them up to fail as well. Likewise, try not to present new instructions as students are getting ready for lunch or dismissal if the information can wait. Instructions are far more effective when they have immediate relevance.

The amount of information we should give out at one time depends on the age and maturity of the students, their experience with our directions, and the complexity of the instructions we offer. In giving oral directions to young students, students who have not had much practice developing their listening skills, or small groups, give directions a step at a time, and wait until the students are ready for the the next step.

Some students simply need a starting point—something concrete from which to begin; there is security in not having to be responsible for everything right off the bat. Examples of this technique include writing from a story starter or creating a drawing from a teacher's beginning mark on a paper. Develop the technique so that eventually students can write story starters or begin their drawings.

Choices within limits—the anthem of the win-win classroom—applies quite clearly to the directions we give. If the limits are too broad, students of any age can be overwhelmed. Sure, there is usually one person in a group who can take a statement like *Construct a meaningful learning experience* and complete the assignment. The rest will flounder.

Concrete boundaries give students the structure they need to begin. We can always offer choices within those limits. In addition to the starting point described on the previous page, we can offer structure by limiting length (one side of a paper), media (a picture made on the computer), expression (written in the present tense, drawn with only one color of ink), content (using all 20 spelling words, people involved in the women's movement during the 1970s), or any number of criteria. Our ultimate objectives for any assignment help determine the amount of structure necessary and choices available. Writing details about tasks to be done or specifying the criteria for a particular assignment saves a great amount of time in repetition of instructions and helps avoid student confusion and mistakes at the same time.

We frequently use directions to express the rules and contingencies necessary in any group. With my first class, I had some reservations about being completely in charge and responsible for the rules, so I tried involving the students in this task. Part of my intention was an honest attempt to acknowledge the students' needs for input and control, and building a positive, win-win classroom environment. I somehow believed that their input would magically involve them in self-management. I was wrong. This exercise killed the entire morning and produced 478 don'ts, nearly a quarter of which had to do with a range of objects the students thought they should not throw in the classroom. I quickly realized that the brunt of enforcement would ultimately rest on my shoulders, and with nearly 500 rules, their list would have certainly kept me hopping. I was eventually able to distill their list into two rules: one about using the pass to leave the room during independent work time and the other about not disrupting the learning or teaching process.

It may come as no surprise that the language we choose in giving oral directions—especially about rules—can also help us encourage responsible cooperation, avoid reinforcing teacher-dependence, and discourage rebelliousness. Since our language and attitude are so closely linked, changing one will most likely change the other. As we commit to a positive, win-win focus, we become increasingly aware of negative tendencies in our words and the tone of our voice. Likewise, as we shift from threats and warnings to promises and contingencies, our attitude mirrors that change.

For example, let's say we want students to put all of the game pieces back in the box before they leave a work area. We can state this need by threatening: *If you don't put everything in the box, I'm taking it out of the center.* We can also promise: *If you put all the game pieces back in the box, I'll leave it in the center.* In both cases, we state the same thing and connect the consequence of their cooperation to the privilege of the game's continual availability. Which would students rather hear? And, as teachers, which would we rather say?

But there is more to this than just sounding pleasant. Although the threat of having the game removed is clearly implied in the promise of leaving the box in the center, the implication of teacher control and responsibility is sharply reduced. In the first example, the game's presence in the center is a function of the teacher's power (external). In the second, it becomes a positive consequence of the student's cooperation (internal)—a subtle, but powerful, difference.

Similarly, the reasons for asking for certain behaviors can either work for or against building responsibility and cooperation. In addition to being clearly understood, instructions (which express what we want or need) must make sense to students. In power-based authority relationships, the reason for doing something is connected to the power of the authority (*Because I said so*) and the punitive consequences of non-compliance (*Do it or else!*). The statement *Do it for me* may sound less powerful, but its implication of conditional approval actually works in the same manner as *Do it or else*.

**Telling students the real, logical, and intrinsic reason for a rule builds commitment and cooperation.**

The win-win classroom operates on the belief that students need not be threatened with deprivations or punitive consequences to be motivated to cooperate. Instead, in 21st century authority relationships, teachers believe the students are capable of making positive choices even when the outcomes are not directly connected with the power of the teacher. For example, *Please put the lids back on the paint jars so the paint doesn't dry out* communicates much more faith in and respect for students than *Put the lids back on the paint jars or you'll never see them again.*

When we ask our students to do something, we usually have a better reason than *because I said so.* Telling them the real, logical, and intrinsic reason for a limit or a rule—so the markers do not dry out, so that we do not disturb anyone on our way down the hall, so that no one trips and falls—builds commitment and cooperation even from rebellious students. These criteria are stated for the benefit of the student and the class as a whole. It has nothing to do with the teacher's needs (although, as part of the group, his or her needs will be served as well). The fact that this approach clearly focuses on the students' needs (what's in it for them or, at least, for the group) accounts for an increase in cooperation. Such an approach only takes a few more seconds; if it builds responsibility, and, at worst, generates cooperation from only half of the students who otherwise would not bother, it's worth it.

Listen to the way contingencies are structured for students. Are they more frequently stated as threats: *If you don't do this, then . . .* or promises *If you do this, then . . . ?* Practically any threat can be restructured into a promise. And as we get to know our students better, we can begin connecting what we want to meaningful positive consequences for them.

Use the following checklist to plan or evaluate the directions for various activities you assign.   **Activity**

Product and/or Behavior:

Objective:

Criteria for successful completion:

Clarity:

Skills or behaviors (cognitive, social, motor) required by this activity which may be new to the students:

Materials or equipment used to complete this activity that may be unfamiliar to the students:

Other considerations (movement within or outside the classroom, need for other facilities or resources):

Presentation (elaborate for each category that applies):

Verbal:

Written:

Illustrated:

Other (taped, signed, another language):

Samples available:

Structure:

Limits/starting point/focus:

Choices available:

Other success-oriented features:

Getting students' attention:

Timeliness [1]:

Small steps:

Logical sequence:

Evaluation Summary:

[1] That is, when are they wound up about something else or is it too far in advance for them to remember.

In what ways were these directions success-oriented?

In what ways did the students have difficulty with the directions?

In what ways might these directions have been even more success-oriented?

Note to self: Next time, remember to . . .

On a separate piece of paper, list three columns. In column one, list five or more desired student behaviors.

In column two, tell how that behavior will benefit you (make your life easier or your job more pleasant).

In column three, tell how that behavior will benefit your students (what's in it for them to cooperate). If possible, state in terms of positive consequences, rather than as a way to avoid a negative consequence. [2]

| Desired behavior | Benefit for me | Benefit for student |
|---|---|---|
|  |  |  |

To what degree have you been successful in announcing limits and criteria before there is a problem or mistake?

Describe a time you did so. In what ways did your behavior contribute to the students' success or positive performance?

To what degree have you been successful in expressing rules and directions positively (for example, turning threats into promises)?

Describe a time you did so. In what ways did your behavior contribute to the students' success or positive performance?

[2] If the only benefit for cooperation is to avoid punishment, criticism, anger, or the teacher's withdrawal, the motivation is external. The positive behavior, therefore, is unlikely to occur on its own if the threat (or power) is removed. If it is difficult to think of positive consequences, it is just because the win-lose power model is so pervasive and familiar. Hang in there.

# 11 Planning and pacing

uccess-oriented planning covers everything from making sure there are enough handouts to determining if the students are conceptually prepared for new material to be presented. The importance of appropriate content is indisputable in instructional planning; attention to details, which is easier to take for granted, is certainly as important. Many otherwise well-planned lessons have been doomed by the simplest omissions, timing mistakes, or errors in judgment. One first-grade teacher saw a terrific art activity fall apart when she realized she had not borrowed enough staplers. Too many kids waiting too long to share too few tools is a formula for disaster.

Consider these examples: a seventh-grade science teacher who planned an entire week's worth of lessons around a shipment of fruit flies that died in transit, or the teacher whose plans to have her kids make their own bingo cards faltered from her students' inexperience with rulers.

Good planning is mostly common sense. Sure, emergencies arise. There are times when the media center ships the wrong video or the one available projector bulb is burned out. In these instances, backup emergency plans can help avoid disaster. But for the most part, thinking through plans can prevent headaches and numerous discipline problems, especially for something new, something you have not done in a while, or something that has never been tried with this particular group.

Anything we can do to minimize confusion, additional movement, off-task time, and interruptions reduces the opportunities for discipline problems to develop. But planning goes beyond the logistical considerations described above; it actually involves what is taught.

At the end of the summer after my first year of teaching, I was offered a job teaching math to the upper five grades in a K-8 school. The staff greeted me with a warning that the eighth graders might be somewhat difficult. The majority of students in this class had not done well in math in years past and would probably not be eager for one more year of failure and frustration.

**This was still math and they were still going to fail as they always had.**

The eighth grade textbook heightened my concerns: these kids were in for a tough year, indeed. After very few pages of review, the book jumped into complex concepts: multiples, factors, ratios, square roots.

*Well,* I thought, *Let's see what these guys remember from seventh grade.* I armed myself with a stack of teacher-made diagnostic exercises, sequenced according to district curriculum goals, to greet the students when they first walked through the door.

When they arrived, it was obvious they did not want to be there. Even the presence of a young enthusiastic teacher did not give them much hope: this was still math, and they were still going to fail as they always had. I shut the door and turned to find 38 hostile, hulking beings, arms folded across chests, eyes glaring and suspicious. Fun.

*OK kids, let's see what you can do.*

I started with the easy stuff: the first assignment tested counting and number sequence. *No grades—just do the best you can.* Each one did OK with this test (I have since had many who did not), which meant that we went on to the next project: Who can add whole numbers? I was not terribly surprised to learn from this test that nearly half of the class could not add if it required regrouping. They performed even worse on the other whole number operations. The few students who mastered the basics were tested on advanced concepts.

As far as planning instruction went, I had only to look at these pre-tests to imagine how most of this group would do on multiples or square roots. I wondered, do I stick to the book and a curriculum that was light years beyond the capabilities of the class, or do I back up and start with what they actually can do? What kind of behavior could I expect from a group of students who could neither understand the lessons nor do the assignments? (This situation was not unique to this particular eighth grade; to somewhat lesser degrees, I faced the same dilemma with other classes as well.)

I felt considerable pressure to teach eighth-grade math to eighth graders, and teach them skills they would be tested on later in a district testing program. But I knew I would only be exposing them to more failures. Their math anxiety, can't-do attitudes, and poor self-concepts did not need any reinforcement. I decided to start wherever needed in order for them to achieve, catching up as best we could. I told this class they needed three things to succeed: a pencil; to show up; and to produce, starting with whatever they could do at that time.

**The challenge was continual: Though we started with something the kids could do, we didn't linger there.**

I was concerned that some of the students were still not in the books after the first few weeks of school. Yet, the pressure was not as strong as it could have been because I had a number of things working in my behalf. I had the diagnostic scores to back up my placements, and while it was likely that a few of these students might never catch on to the most complex concepts, every child in that room made tremendous progress in a very short period of time.

This example underscores the following: Our greatest strides in developing win-win relationships, self-managing student behavior, and a positive classroom climate can be sadly undermined by teaching content that is poorly matched to student abilities. If it sounds like the alternative makes it too easy, keep in mind that the challenge was continual. Even though we started with something the kids could do, we did not linger there. From the first, the lessons demanded stretching beyond the comfort of previous achievements. Aside from a few practice laps, each successful trip around the track meant a higher hurdle to clear next time around.

The increased success the students experienced was engaging: overall attitudes improved and off-task behavior was at a minimum. Students were taking risks, trying new things, and beginning to believe that they could actually succeed in this class. Furthermore, I received notes from parents, pleased and surprised to see their children bringing their books home, enthusiastic about math for the first time ever!

Without the belief that success is within reach and the willingness to go after it, learning will not take place. The notion of *toughening them up* by letting them fail is a rather sadistic holdover from power-oriented, win-lose relationships. Students have plenty of opportunities to mess up. Deliberately setting them up to fail is far more likely to slow them down, if not stop them cold. If we really want our students to make it in a tough world, they will be far better served by practicing success than failure.

And what about next year? Some of those eighth graders were promoted into ninth grade math classes without some of the math skills of the eighth grade curriculum. But they had made progress, and at least they had mastered the skills from elementary math. One more year of failure and frustration at the eighth grade level would hardly have made them more successful the following year.

**Planning addresses what the kids can do, where their interests lie, and how to best reinforce student commitment and belief in self.**

We need to be careful that concern for next year does not throw our intentions off balance. It is important to prepare kids to succeed with success and help them build the confidence and flexibility that will enable them to handle difficulties more effectively.

Success-oriented planning leads to success-oriented instruction. In addition to thinking through the details and logistics of specific activities, planning also addresses what the kids can do, where their interests lie, and how to best reinforce the students' commitment, risk-taking, perseverance, and belief in their own potential for achievement.

Perhaps the greatest benefit of success orientation in a classroom is its ability to sharply reduce instances of disruption, confusion, frustration, conflict, and wasted time. Success orientation and win-win relationships will not completely eliminate problems, but they will certainly help prevent a large number of them. We will still be faced with the task of motivating a nondisruptive student, recognizing cooperation, or intervening when a misbehavior occurs—and need different tools for each. These situations will be discussed in greater detail in the following section.

Here is a checklist for success-oriented planning to evaluate    **Activity**
activities and lessons before you implement them:

\_\_\_\_\_ Do I have enough materials?

\_\_\_\_\_ How will I distribute them?

\_\_\_\_\_ What changes in furniture or room arrangement will I
need to make?

\_\_\_\_\_ Do students have to move?

\_\_\_\_\_ How can I make this transition as smooth as possible?

\_\_\_\_\_ What will I do during this activity?

\_\_\_\_\_ How free will I be to help answer questions or monitor
behavior?

\_\_\_\_\_ What materials, rules, and arrangements have I made
to help the students solve problems without bothering
me?

\_\_\_\_\_ When is this activity planned?

\_\_\_\_\_ Is that the best time for this lesson?

\_\_\_\_\_ Do they need time to cool down from their last class?

\_\_\_\_\_ Is it too close to the weekend/holiday to introduce
something new?

\_\_\_\_\_ What else might I need to contend with or compensate
for?

\_\_\_\_\_ What alternatives are available?

\_\_\_\_\_ What are they most likely to misunderstand?

\_\_\_\_\_ What else do I need to go over?

\_\_\_\_\_ Do the students need to practice anything first?

\_\_\_\_\_ What do they need to do, have, or get before they can
begin?

\_\_\_\_\_ What are the things that can go wrong, and what do I do
if any of these actually happens?

What's "Plan B" if this one flops altogether?
Now, repeat all of the above for Plan B.

Design a chart with four columns.

In column one, tell what sort of back-up materials and plans you have for those occasions on which a particular lesson does not work, the materials you ordered do not come in on time, or the kids finish in half the time you anticipated.

In column two, tell where the materials are located.

In column three, tell if the materials are ready for use (if not, note what has to be done).

In column four, describe any special instructions, materials, or preparation the students will need in order to do these back-up activities. If the students can get started as soon as they receive the materials, simply mark this column *independent.*

| Back-up materials | Location | Ready for use | Special instructions, preparations, or materials |
|---|---|---|---|
|  |  |  |  |

These materials and activities can be especially valuable when they are available for a substitute who may have difficulty following your plans; pulling everything together for a more complex lesson; substituting in the middle of a unit; or getting the kids' cooperation. Make it easy for the substitute to succeed, too! If you feel that these particular activities may not be appropriate, pull together a separate set of emergency plans and materials to leave in a substitute's survival folder. It is a safe bet your efforts will be appreciated and lead to a better experience for the sub, the kids, and you when you return.

Section Three

# Building Responsibility and Self-management

# 12 Motivation and contingencies

One year, Billy, a new student, came to my fourth-grade class during the second week of school. He was shy and polite and could entertain himself for hours without bothering a soul. Billy also refused to do any work; he neither participated in discussions nor touched any of the assigned paper-and-pencil activities. He was a very pleasant kid to have around, but I was not willing to accept his presence as merely ornamental.

Reminders, threats, and negative consequences were unproductive, and the call home did not generate the sort of support that might have shaken Billy loose from his resistance to schoolwork. Talking to Billy revealed that he was aware that he could not be promoted from a class in which he did not do anything; in fact he seemed quite content to while away the year counting the holes in the ceiling tile.

I told him that I would continue to give him the day's assignments and be available for help. I would not, however, continue to nag, threaten, or force—these efforts had not only been frustrating and ineffective, they were taking away time I could spend with other students. I was not happy with the choice Billy had made, nor with my inability to turn him around. His success in fourth grade was far more important to me than it seemed to be to him. But for the moment, I could only offer him chances to change his mind.

Two days later, the office called my room, asking me to please send certain forms down by lunchtime. I had just finished collecting the materials they wanted and looked around for a messenger. Everyone seemed to be busy with something—except Billy, who was, at that moment, having a staring contest with a box of chalk. He was certainly available. Still, privilege had its contingencies: Billy could take the papers to the office if he wanted, as soon as his work was finished. To my amazement, Billy ran up to me 15 minutes later, work in hand. Everything looked fine. It was the first time I had ever seen his writing. Without even thinking about it, I had stumbled upon magic: Billy would do anything to get out of the room!

> **I had stumbled upon magic: Billy would do anything to get out of the room.**

Motivation means recognizing that behaviors are chosen, and that human beings behave in the way that is the most need-fulfilling. Let's look at this question from an adult perspective. Think of a household (or classroom) chore that you really detest doing, but do anyway. Now explain why you perform such a distasteful task. Think of as many reasons as you can. (If one of your reasons is *because I should do it*, specify the reason you think you should.)

Chore:
I do it because:

These reasons tell what is in it for you when you do something you really dislike. These are the options that are more need-fulfilling than avoiding the task you specified, and they only motivate you when they are, indeed, more need-fulfilling or more important than putting off doing the chore.

For example, let us say you chose *cleaning the bathroom* as something you hate to do. And let us say that you, on occasion, do clean the bathroom for the following reasons:
• Because your roommate nags you if you don't.
• Because you are afraid of the stuff that grows on the shower tile.
• Because company is coming.

And let's imagine that your roommate is out of town for a week, that the shower tile still looks clean, and your company cancels at the last minute. Are those reasons (avoiding the nagging, the stuff, or your company's shock and discomfort) as compelling as they might ordinarily be? Chances are you will put off this chore until one or another of those options becomes more pressing.

When we do something we really don't want to do, we choose the option because doing so is more need-fulfilling than the alternatives. There has to be something in it for us—whether it is personal satisfaction, avoidance of punishment or deprivation, or some type of fulfillment; otherwise we simply do not choose to do it.

Likewise, when people cooperate with us, they do what we want because doing so serves their purposes in some way. Perhaps they are trying to make us happy, gain our approval, get us off their backs, obligate us for some later time, validate their suffering, or make themselves feel worthwhile, simply because it feels good to them. There is always some payoff, some need-fulfilling positive consequence, behind their cooperation. Being skilled at motivating others means paying close attention to that very issue: What can they gain by doing what we want?

Motivating our students works the same way. Getting them to do something we want them to do means we have to find an option that the students find more appealing and important than avoiding what we want. A number of options are open to us; anything that is meaningful to our students can be used as a motivator. Although a teacher's approval or disapproval can be very effective with some students, using a teacher response as a primary motivator takes us back to building obedience and teacher-dependence. In a win-win classroom, where students feel accepted, welcome, and worthwhile even on less productive days, motivators will more likely take the form of some pleasurable activity instead.

**We need to offer a pleasurable outcome to motivate students for one reason: it works.**

Such contingencies are nothing new. Grandma had this one down when she said we could have our dessert after we finished our vegetables. Either way, it was our choice. But if we really hated the vegetable, it didn't matter what the dessert was. And if we really loved the dessert, we probably would have eaten anything to get it. Regardless of the choice we made, the only thing at stake was dessert—not Grandma's love, approval, or temper.

Is this a bribe? Sure—that's how motivation operates. The echo from industrial-era authority relationships will question why we need to offer a pleasurable outcome to students for doing what they simply should do. The answer is: it works. We expect something for the work we do, whether it be our enjoyment of teaching, the satisfaction of knowing we are shaping young lives, the paycheck we get at the end of the month, or the fact that our job gets us out of the house once in a while. Why shouldn't kids want some meaningful consequence for what they choose to do?

In addition, seeing the positive outcomes of their cooperative behavior helps reinforce the students' responsibility for their choices. Experiencing a connection between positive choices and outcomes strengthens the students' recognition of the cause-and-effect relationship between the behaviors they choose and what happens to them as a result of their choices. Rewarding consequences also reinforces the students' belief in their ability to positively affect their own lives.

*Shoulds* do not teach self-management: Doing something simply because one *should* reflects obedience and people-pleasing; it rarely requires responsible decision-making or connecting personal needs and probable outcomes.

What about *learning for learning's sake?* Don't we all want our students to work for the love of learning? Of course we do. (Is there anyone easier to motivate than the student who comes to our classroom with a burning desire for knowledge?) But surely these aspirations are not simply for a teacher's benefit. Such students are also functioning at the highest levels of need-fulfillment.

If we look at the range of needs that motivate people, we find a hierarchy in which the more basic needs must be satisfied before higher-level needs. A hungry student, for example, may not be too concerned with whether or not her handwriting is improving until she gets some food in her stomach. Once the basic physiological needs are satisfied, however, students seek fulfillment at a higher level.

In a win-lose classroom, the frequent existence of arbitrary power and absence of trust are likely to keep kids striving to meet their needs for safety. These students rarely take risks or go beyond the bare minimum in order to avoid confrontation and keep from drawing attention to themselves. (Even those vying for positions of power and acceptance among their peers, and the ones trying to be teacher's pet, place this goal above learning, simply to assure their safety in the teacher-student relationship.) Getting to higher-level needs, including the need for knowledge and learning, requires that students feel safe. A success-oriented classroom not only allows safety needs to be met, but also acknowledges higher-level needs for acceptance and belonging, success and achievement, and input and control. In a win-win environment, learning for learning's sake stands a good chance of coming about.

And yet, doing anything for its own sake *must be perceived* as pleasurable and rewarding in some way. Even in the ideal environment, this goal may be beyond the reach of many students. Therefore, a task that is perceived as unfulfilling may have to be connected to something meaningful and immediate to build positive patterns. The promise of possible long-term results might not do it.

**A task that is perceived as unfulfilling has to be connected to something meaningful and positive.**

Billy's love of wandering the halls (what he wanted) gave him an initial reason for doing his classwork (what I wanted). For this student, unwilling to take even the slightest risk, the availability of something even more need-fulfilling than avoiding the task was absolutely essential. Access to a positive outcome—something that Billy perceived as valuable— gave him the drive that all the threats, lectures, and nagging did not achieve. It was a start, and one that created a positive association with the entire experience of being and working in fourth grade. As that connection became more firmly established, the need for the external, unrelated reward died out.

Likewise, simply hearing that they would need basic math skills to balance a checkbook and plan a budget had little motivational value to those eighth graders who had neither a checkbook nor a budget. The only way to break the inertia was to connect their initial attempts to some immediate, positive outcomes. That might mean working a math reinforcement puzzle, creating a new bulletin board, grading one's own assignment, helping another student choose an enrichment activity, receiving a sticker, or moving on to the next skill at the completion of a task. Each time a student experienced the positive outcomes of his or her cooperative choosing, the connection was reinforced. As the bond grew stronger, the behavior became increasingly internalized and habitual.

A high school teacher was assigned late in the year to a large group of high-risk and extremely hostile seniors after the original teacher and several replacements had quit. The new teacher could barely get their attention, and when she handed out an assignment, every student in the room tore it up. *We never pass anything, anyhow,* one declared.

Only somewhat discouraged, she returned the next day with the same assignment and announced, *If you turn it in with your name on it, you get a C.* Most of the students simply shook their heads and tore the papers up again, although six or seven defiantly scrawled their names across the paper and turned them in. The next day she came back with their graded papers, as promised, with a C for having turned something in, and another stack of work to give them. Although still suspicious, they suddenly gave her their attention. *If you can get a C for writing your name, imagine what you can get for doing some work!*

It was a start. And eventually—between making success possible and providing other need-fulfilling options for co-operation—she hooked every kid in the class. As the trust relationship grew, students were willing to take greater risks. The hurdles also got higher: after a short time, it took more than writing one's name on the paper to get a passing grade.

As with Billy and the kids in my math class, staying on task, attempting new content, and progressing through the requirements of the curriculum eventually became the rewards. Sure, there were students who gained competence and still did not love the subject area. There are some activities and chores that may never be rewarding, no matter how well we can do them! But as achievement eroded resistance, students became learners. If they did not all find a love of learning in that class, at least it was an invitation to finding it elsewhere.

We promise students an A if they do their work, but there are always a few students who are not motivated by grades. We allow students to go out to recess, but there are always a few who would just as soon stay inside. On the other hand, there is always someone who would do anything for the privilege of straightening out the teacher's desk, grading the spelling tests, or—as in Billy's case—running a stack of papers downstairs. But what about those students who do not seem to be motivated by anything?

**Many awards and outcomes that are valuable to students might not be terribly attractive to us.**

Moving away from factory-era thinking means we try to become more aware and appreciative of students' needs and increasingly creative about the types of contingencies offered. Because many rewards and outcomes that are valuable to students would probably not be terribly attractive to us, it is easy to overlook some great motivators. For example, few teachers would go out of their way to grade papers for someone else. Offer that privilege to students though, and watch eyes light up. The same goes for a chance to make a ditto, wash the blackboard, use carbon paper or ball-point pens, load the projector, or engage in any number of cleanup chores.

I once asked a fifth grader to get a box of science equipment out of my car. When she returned, she put the box on my desk and shook her head. *Your car is a mess,* she said.

She was right; it was rare that my car was not littered by papers, plans, materials, textbooks, and at least a few fast-food wrappers. *Would you like to clean it out?* I asked.

*Ooo! Can I?*

(*Hmm,* I wondered. *Do you clean bathrooms?*)

Now, I doubt I would have thought of car-cleaning as a reward, but the task was obviously more attractive to her than it was to me. It is also hard to see *more work* as motivating, yet enrichment and content-related activities can be very appealing to students, especially if there are choices available or if *more work* clearly indicates advancement. (Ever notice how students in basal readers tend to really perk up through the last unit so they can get into the next, more difficult book?)

Learning about our students, through simple conversation or formal assessment instruments, can lead us to significant insights. For example, another student who refused to work was referred for a variety of testing procedures. One of the supervisors happened to strike up a conversation with the student during which time the student revealed that his favorite thing about school was the janitor. The supervisor approached the custodian and was able to set up a contingency by which the student could help out after his work was done.

When the results of a learning styles survey [1] indicated that the majority of my students preferred working with a partner, greater mobility, and sound in the enviroment, I offered one or more of those options during certain activities *as long as the students continued to perform.* This survey also revealed that my most difficult reading group was made up of students who preferred afternoons and evenings to mornings. Our reading periods had been scheduled early in the day when these students were not at their best. It took some juggling, but switching that group to the afternoon made a tremendous difference in the students' attention, participation, retention, performance, and achievement levels. In each case, attempting to meet student needs paid off for me as well. Win-win.

Sometimes a contingency can be as valuable a learning experience in itself as any classroom activity. One year, our kindergarten teacher felt a bit overwhelmed by some of the management and housekeeping responsibilities involved in keeping a large, full-day group going. I offered to ask some of my upper-grade students to help. My students required little

**Learning about students can lead to significant insights: one student revealed that his favorite thing about school was the janitor!**

coaxing and began helping out, as always, when their seat-work was done. Their first tasks were fairly mechanical—mixing paint or covering tables for art activities; helping the younger students open their milk cartons, zip their jackets, or get in line; or helping the teacher with organization and cleanup chores. They quickly began offering to help out in centers, play games, put on puppet shows, or review colors, numbers, letters, and various other concepts. Some of my weakest and most resistant readers volunteered to read stories to the kindergarten kids. This was a real *I can* experience that was ultimately reflected in their classroom performance.

**It was an *I can* experience that was eventually reflected in performance.**

We were able to get every upper-grade student involved as a helper. Students who had never done homework before were asking to do their independent work at home so they could go down and help. Amazingly, some even asked to give up recess to work in the kindergarten!

My students were suddenly doing larger amounts of increasingly difficult work. Because the privilege demanded that the helpers stay caught up and out of trouble in their classes, overall discipline was greatly improved. At the same time, their successes in the kindergarten and opportunities to model were beginning to show in their interactions and behaviors with their peers, other teachers, and even at home[2]. Self-concepts and general attitudes improved; attendance was up, detentions were down. Students who had rarely, if ever, demonstrated anything in the way of self-management, were beginning to behave more responsibly and with greater self-control. One student even walked away from a fight, took the hall pass, and stood outside the door until he had a chance to cool down. This was unheard of. I did not even have to open my mouth! School had become more enjoyable and rewarding for everyone, and I was amazed at the amount of time I had for instruction because I was not involved in disciplining students.

One caution in looking for meaningful motivators: When we attempt to determine *what is in it for them*, we need to differentiate between the assumed or projected benefits (which usually reflect our value system) and the actual benefits (what the students perceive as a positive outcome). For example, graduation from fourth grade was meaningful and important to me; but it was not meaningful enough to Billy to motivate him to participate in class. We, as adults, often appreciate the long-range benefits of the things we ask our students to do far better than they. Some of our more mature students *may* have also made that connection. Still, these students may have the rhetoric down, particularly if they are good at teacher-pleasing, but they probably will not actually be motivated by positive consequences beyond their immediate experiences. For the most part, the more immediate and personally meaningful the positive outcome, the more likely the cooperation.

For example, a student is more likely to be motivated to write a coherent paragraph in order to print it out on the computer this afternoon than to make himself more attractive in the job market ten years from now. In most cases, we are correct in our commitment to the importance of whatever it is we want our students to do. But unless there is also an immediate or foreseeable positive consequence for the students, in most cases our commitment will do us little good. Even adults find immediate and personal consequences more compelling than long-range possibilities. (Would our efforts at dieting, for example, be more successful if we could actually see a difference each time we turned down a doughnut?) One student might write her term paper the day it is assigned; she finds it fulfilling to do so. Another might put it off until a grade, raise, or job depends on it—and then may still let it go if those payoffs aren't as important as the other things that kept him from writing the paper in the first place.

**All students do not have similar personalities and work habits; all DO appreciate having their individuality recognized.**

Industrial-era thinking sounds another concern: *If you let Billy take a message to the office, do you have to let everybody take things down when they finish their work?* Of course not. In that class, some kids might work for the grade, some to advance to the next assignment, others for some structured free time, and a few because they really like and usually do well in that particular subject. Sending them on an errand as motivation would have been pointless. Likewise, I had students who found no fascination with running around the school on missions for me. Attempting to motivate them with messenger privileges would have been futile. All students do not have similar personalities, tastes, and work habits; all *do* appreciate having their individuality recognized.

Let's go back to the chore you were thinking about earlier in this chapter. Suppose that for some reason I feel that it is important for you to practice this chore in some different setting, say at my house or in my classroom. Hypothetically speaking, what would it take to motivate you now? Try to think of at least five outcomes (rewards) that would motivate you. Be specific: if you say *money*, for example, how much?

In workshops, I pose the example of coming to clean my

bathroom. The range of responses from other teachers gives strong support for the differences in personal needs and the need for different motivators for different people. Some offer to come and clean it for nothing—evidence of either their (admitted) need to please or the fact that some chores are simply less obnoxious to some than to others. Some ask for unspecified amounts of money, but when I offer a nice, shiny dime, most of the hands go down. Some will do it for ten dollars; others won't budge for less than a few hundred.

Still others would not clean my bathroom for a thousand dollars, they claim; although they might agree to an offer to write their lesson plans for the rest of the year. Various others, originally resistant, have relented for a great home-cooked meal, a weekend without their kids, having me do their ironing or dishes for a week, getting out of grading papers for a month, or five pounds of chocolate. One teacher said she would do my bathroom and more if I would take the time to write her a note telling her that I appreciated what she had done!

See, we all have our price and there is always a choice. In motivating cooperation—with kids or adults—it is almost always worth our while to offer something they cannot refuse. And that does not have to cost us a thing.

[1] Dunn, K. and Dunn, R. *Educator's Self-Teaching Guide to Individualized Instruction*. MJ: Parker Publishing Co., Inc., 1975.

[2] Bluestein, J. *Building Responsible Learning Behaviors through Peer Interaction*. Unpublished doctoral dissertation, University of Pittsburgh, 1980.

# Guidelines for Setting Contingencies

- Use contingencies (outcomes) that are meaningful and important to the student to encourage him or her to adopt a particular behavior he or she is not currently demonstrating.

- Contingencies can also help prevent disruptive behaviors; however, other strategies will be suggested for discouraging negative behavior or reinforcing performance, growth, and existing positive behavior.

- Offer contingencies for completion of specific, limited tasks. For example, *If you finish this worksheet by the time the show starts* or *If you stay in your seat until this page is completed* is preferable to offering a reward for good behavior. Reward accomplishment—not obedience.

- State contingencies in a positive manner, using language such as *if/then* or *as soon as*. Don't include negative consequences *(and if you don't . . . )* when presenting a contingency. The lack of access to the positive outcome, implicit in the *if/then* statement, should be the only negative consequence of non-cooperation. Avoid communicating the contingency as a threat of punishment or deprivation.

- Keep initial demands small, short, and simple, and rewards small, immediate, and frequent. Raise the hurdles gradually and decrease the reward over time. (For a student like Billy, you might start with an errand after each assignment he completes, working toward finishing the morning's work, and then the full day. Eventually, verbal reinforcement with sporadic opportunities to run an errand should be sufficient to maintain the desired behavior.)

- Be clear about what you want the student to do, as well as what the student will get to do in return.

- Get a sense of what your students perceive as meaningful through dialogue, observation, or assessment. (Use interest inventories, learning styles surveys, sociometric questionnaires, or time-on-task assessments.)

- Select only win-win contingencies (those that will not hurt, deprive, or inconvenience someone else).

- Make contingencies available on a non-competitive basis. Rather than offering copies of the dinosaur word-search puzzle to the first row that's finished, make the puzzle available to every student who completes the assignment.

- If your contingency can only be available to one or two students at a time (such as washing the board or emptying the trash), make sure the other students have access to those privileges at some other times and that they have other rewards available to them in the meantime.

- Although it would be silly, if not impossible, to hide the fact that we're pleased when our students do what we ask, try to avoid using conditional approval or acceptance as a motivator.

- Tokens and stickers can be effective, even with older students, if limited to very specific tasks. Avoid offering tokens more than once or twice a day, if that. The management alone can drive you crazy. Think about activities you can offer instead.

- Use contingencies that help build responsible behavior and, if possible, reinforce content. Examples include enrichment activities, structured free time, grading one's own papers, peer helping or tutoring, access to a film or extra trip to the library, filing, or housekeeping chores.

- Activities that involve cooking or food can be valuable motivators, but avoid offering food as a reward—especially sweets. (If you have the resources and inclination to bring in food for a hungry child or as a treat for your class, that's fine. But as a contingency, a quick snack has far fewer long-term effects than a privilege.)

- If possible, state the contingency once. Avoid nagging and reminding. If the student makes poor choices, lack of access to the contingency is a far more effective consequence than a lecture.

- If a student does not complete the task or does not seem to be motivated by the contingency you have offered, consider the following:
  — Can the student do what I have asked him/her to do?
  — Is the student overwhelmed by the amount of work or time required for access to the contingency? Do I need to back up a bit?
  — Is the contingency meaningful to the student? What else might work?

- If the student does not complete the task because he or she is just having an off day, leave the door open for access at another time: *Let's try again this afternoon (or tomorrow)*. Accept the student, even if his or her behavior is not acceptable.

**Exercise**    On another paper, draw a chart with four columns, such as the one depicted below.

In column one, list some of the behaviors you ask of your students.

In column two, tell what's in it for you if the students perform each behavior you have listed in column one.

In column three, identify the long-term objectives for the students (what you feel the students will get out of performing each behavior).

In column four, identify the immediate payoffs for the students (what they get or perceive as a meaningful outcome for performing each behavior).

| Student behaviors | What's in it for you | Long-term objectives | Immediate payoffs |
|---|---|---|---|
|  |  |  |  |

Now go back and look at column 4. Of the responses you marked, how many:

\_\_\_\_\_ were related to teacher approval or avoidance of punishment?

\_\_\_\_\_ offered tokens, tickets, stickers, or food?

\_\_\_\_\_ offered higher-interest activities upon completion of the task?

\_\_\_\_\_ offered choices related to the task itself?

\_\_\_\_\_ were left blank?


In what ways are your motivational strategies successful:

— in getting your students to do what you want?


— in building responsibility, initiative, and self-management?

In what ways have you investigated your students' needs and preferences? If you think you need more information, take some time out to collect some data before continuing this exercise. You may find some of the following strategies helpful:

- Develop a *fill-in* type of inventory, with questions such as *After school I like to* _____, *The best thing about school is* _____ or *I wish I could take a class in* _____. Students can write in answers, dictate answers, or interview one another.

- Develop an inventory with a number of hobbies, sports, types of music or TV shows, types of stories, after-school activities and so on. Students check activities they have tried and/or evaluate their interest in each item on a scale of 1 to 5.

- Administer a commercial inventory of interests or learning styles.

- Discuss the students' interests in a formal discussion or values activity.

- Discuss the students' interests informally, as a matter of conversation.

- Discuss students' interests with their parents or other teachers.

- Ask your colleagues what has worked for them in motivating particular students.

Design a chart similar to the one below. Plan enough space to devote one line to each student.

If you are working with several classes, you may wish to select one class (or group of students) that has been the most difficult to motivate.

Write the students' names in the left-hand column and in the space to the right of their names jot down topics or activities of interest to each individual. A list of interests might include: horses, cooking, comic books, Sesame Street, mysteries, drawing, working with Melissa, grading papers, reading to younger students, swimming, airplanes, dancing, playing soccer, watching the Steelers, making jewelry, and so on. Add to this list as you learn more about each student.

| Student | Motivators |
|---------|------------|
|         |            |
|         |            |
|         |            |
|         |            |
|         |            |

From this information, what other kinds of activity-type motivators might work in your classroom (which you are willing and able to provide and that your students might find need-fulfilling)?

What changes would you propose in your motivational strategies?

Before completing this exercise, try implementing some of the changes you proposed above for at least three to four weeks.

Describe the impact of the contingencies you
implemented on:

Student cooperation:

Student self-management, responsible behavior:

Student attitude, self-concept, initiative:

# 13    Cooperation and choices

**M**s. Cahill, a student teacher, was trying to get her seventh-grade math students to warm up with ten subtraction review problems in the first few minutes of class. After two days, the students had used up most of the class period and still had not finished the review work. Ms. Cahill collected completed assignments from only a handful of students and never did manage to get to the new material she intended to teach after the planned ten-minute review period.

The next day, instead of ten problems, the students walked in to find fifteen on the board. Ms. Cahill announced that they could choose any ten they wanted to do. Guess what? Before the class let out, every student had completed at least ten problems; amazingly, over half had done all fifteen. The difference was in choosing and the *power* it gave students; just having a choice was enormously motivating. The next few days were devoted to improving their time, but most important, a pattern for cooperation and on-task behavior had been established.

The importance of offering choices became apparent to me, but for an entirely different reason. After the learning center fiasco (described in Chapter 7) that exposed my fifth graders' lack of independent learning skills, I decided to try something simpler. The next morning, I came in armed with two stacks of worksheets, one for math, the other for spelling. I distributed them and told the students that both needed to be done before recess, which was an hour away. Immediately, one of the students asked which one they should do first.

*It doesn't matter,* I answered. *Just get them both done.* The class was dumbfounded. They looked uneasily at one another and back to me. *Well, which one should we do first?*

*I don't care as long as they both get done.*

I was amazed at the difficulty the students were having, not in determining whether to do math or spelling first—but in determining how to decide. They were lost. OK, I could understand how asking them to self-manage in small groups, do complex activities independently, and design their own projects might have been overwhelming. But how could they possibly be stupefied by two dittos?

By this point, a few students had begun to eye their papers. One or two had actually started working on one sheet or the other. A few, however, appeared stricken. One student was on the verge of tears. I couldn't stand it anymore: I asked her if she wanted me to help her choose (which, incidentally, is a choice in itself). She sniffed and nodded.

*Why don't you do the math assignment?* I suggested.

She hesitated. Almost imperceptibly she answered, *I'd rather do the spelling.* (This was another one of those moments when I wondered why I had gone into teaching.) Later that day I realized that this trauma was part of her learning the skill of decision-making. And I also thought about the number of truly consequential decisions these kids currently faced or would be facing in the not-too-distant future: Should I finish school? Should I drink this beer? Should I enlist in the Army? Should I get in the back seat of this guy's car? How would they fare on the big questions if they were flabbergasted by something as simple as which ditto to do first?

As if I didn't have enough to cover that year, now I had to teach decision-making, too. I was just beginning to appreciate the fact that learning to choose was a skill as much as any other I would have to teach, one that needed to be taught from the ground up and practiced and refined along the way. Well, it seemed as good a place as any to begin, and I knew

**Learning to choose is a skill just like any other. It needs to be taught from the ground up and practiced and refined along the way.**

that unless I helped them develop and practice that skill, I would never see the kind of independent learning behaviors my plans would require.

The practice of offering choices to our students serves several purposes, including reinforcing decision-making skills, addressing the students' needs for input and control in their lives, and motivating work completion through empowerment. This experience is quite different from the results of simply telling students what to do. The power behind a command is in itself likely to provoke resistance. We defuse that power and put the responsibility back on the student when we switch from telling to asking. (At no point are we asking the students if they want to do the work or not.) Certainly in a do-it-or-else assignment, there is an implicit option for students to say no. Offering choices focuses the students away from yes or no to two or more different yes options.

**We defuse the power in a command and put responsibility back on students when we switch from telling to asking.**

Choices also generate commitment from students. Had I simply handed those two papers to the students insisting that they do Math first, I would have probably seen some students comply, although there would have been a few who would have argued for Spelling just to be different. Either way, the only person committed to the activity would have been me. In offering them a choice, the second they put their pencils to the papers, they made a commitment.

Offering choices teaches a lot about win-win and negotiation, too. For example, I had never been terribly creative about the spelling lessons I assigned, and had a student register an early complaint about the required practice of writing each word five times. *This is stupid!* Donald announced.

OK, so it was not my best assignment, but the repetition did seem to help some of the kids. *Well, Donald, the whole idea here is to learn these words. If you have a better way to do it, go ahead.*

The next day, Donald came in with a crossword puzzle using nearly all of the 20 words, with definitions he had made up himself. He had also created a word search puzzle (which I was free, he informed me, to duplicate for the rest of the class) and written a story using the entire list. Of course, he knew these words inside out.

I imagined that if that freedom worked for Donald, it might just spur the rest of the class. So the following week, instead of the traditional no-choice program we had been following, I came in with a list of ten possible activities, including the oldies-but-goodies like *Write each word five times* and the assignments in the book. I also included the ideas Donald had created and left Number 10 as *Design your own activity.*

Each student was to choose any four of the ten activities. These choices allowed the students to accommodate their personal learning needs. Some preferred the security of the sequence we had always used; others preferred the challenge of the newer choices. Others skipped around, trying one set of activities one week, another the next. And Number 10 inspired some projects that were far more complex than anything I could have dreamed up for them to do.

Productivity was up—not just from the kids who had always done well and had become bored in spelling—but also from students who had never done much in the subject. The students were taking more responsibility and initiative for their own learning, and everyone was practicing decision-making. The addition of choice made the tasks more attractive, bringing us one step closer to that precious goal: *learning for learning's sake.* Perhaps even more important, however, was the opportunity to model flexibility and reinforce win-win: *Your needs (for freedom and creativity) are important and so are mine (for your performance and learning). We can both get what we want without anyone suffering.*

Well-constructed choices have two components: options that satisfy the students' need for control and limits that satisfy their need for structure. In the example, *Decide which of these two dittos to do first,* the students control the sequence, while the teacher controls the tasks. True, there isn't much flexibility here, but this type of choice is a perfect starting point for students who have not had much of a chance to practice decision-making skills. Other simple choices might propose that the students decide which two worksheets out of three to do, what color paper to use for an art project, or whether they want to display their projects or take them home.

As students build confidence in their decision-making capabilities, we can ease up on the limits, offer more options or increasingly complex ones. We might ask them to decide whether they would prefer practicing a math skill by doing a page in the book, a cross-number puzzle, or a skill card in a commercial kit. They might choose how to arrange certain materials in a display, select a topic and design for a new bulletin board, or visit a learning center during independent work time. As they progress, they might decide whether to present a report in written, drawn, constructed, or video format.

**The addition of choice made the tasks more attractive, bringing us closer to that precious goal: *Learning for learning's sake!!***

Eventually, we give students options that demand even higher levels of self-management and responsibility: ask them to select a work space for a given period of time; decide whether to stop talking or leave the group; or whether they need more practice on a particular skill. One teacher offered a restless bunch of second graders a choice between a one-minute break immediately or a five-minute break when they finished the lesson in ten minutes.

Once we start questioning the motivation for the tasks we assign in terms of the students' needs (what is in it for them), we can begin to find all sorts of options we can use in offering choices to our students. And as the limits expand and options increase in number and complexity, students gain a stake, not only in the classroom, but in their learning and personal growth as well.

But even Ms. Cahill had some concerns about this strategy, successful as it was. Does the practice of offering choices cause children to expect a choice about everything? By concentrating on what is in it for them, am I teaching them to be selfish? Am I putting them in charge?

Offering choices in no way undermines an authority relationship. Only in a win-lose classroom does empowering students mean disempowering teachers. The adult still decides what is and is not negotiable. Notice that Ms. Cahill did not ask the students to choose whether they wanted to do math or not, she simply found a way to offer the students some input in the situation. And as to the issue of selfishness, these win-win techniques foster *self-care* that is, meeting one's own needs without hurting, disturbing, or depriving anyone else. That is the kind of *selfishness* that enables children to learn to act in their own best interests when an adult is not around to tell them what to do.

**Exercise**    On a separate sheet of paper, list the types of choices that are available to your students. Clarify the options you offer by describing the choices in the left-hand column and the limits on the right. (If you are not offering many choices in your learning environment, describe some choices you could offer. Then, take a few weeks to try out some of these choices before coming back to complete the other questions.)

| Choices | Limits |
|---------|--------|
|         |        |

How many of the choices you offer relate to:

_____ time or sequence (order of activities, when the students can do the work)?

_____ location (where in the school or classroom the students can work on the activity)?

_____ social preferences (selecting a partner to work with, working alone)?

_____ content (choosing their own topics, selecting activities or topics from a given list, designing their own projects)?

_____ type of presentation (oral; written; drawn; using a computer, audio or video equipment; other media)?

_____ other?

In what ways have your students had difficulty making choices?

What have you done or what are you doing to remedy those difficulties?

In what ways are the choices helping to:

— establish positive teacher-student relationships and a win-win classroom environment?

— generate cooperation and productivity?

— build responsibility, self-management, empowerment, and independence?

— develop decision-making and problem-solving skills?

— encourage win-win behaviors such as flexibility and negotiation?

— encourage learning for learning's sake?

What other choices can you offer your students?

# Guidelines for Offering Choices

- Choices, like contingencies, are motivational tools that encourage cooperation through input and empowerment, build responsibility and commitment, and communicate respect for the needs of all concerned. Offer choices to encourage the student to perform a particular behavior he or she is not currently demonstrating.

- Choices can also help prevent disruptive behaviors; however, other strategies will be suggested for handling negative behavior and reinforcing performance, growth, and existing positive behavior.

- Present options in a positive manner. Be careful that the choice doesn't end up spoken as *Do it or else.*

- Be honest. Make sure that all options you offer are acceptable. Avoid setting the students up to choose the *right* option or read your mind. There should be no wrong choices—if you don't want the student to choose something, don't make it an option. (If you want them to do the outline first, offer sequence options about the other activities—after the outline is finished.)

- Make sure the choices you offer are clear and specific. Stating an option such as *Select a meaningful learning activity* leaves room for broad interpretations. Instead, define choices with clearly stated limits: *Select one meaningful learning activity from the five on the board* is much easier for the student to understand and achieve.

- Start simple. If a student is having difficulty making decisions, it may be that there are too many options or that the limits are too broad or unclear.

- If a student is having difficulty with even a simple choice, add another limit by asking him or her to choose within a certain amount of time (after which you get to help the student choose). Be patient. Young students and especially conditioned order-takers need time and practice to develop confidence in their abilities to choose.

- Increase options as the students can handle them, either by widening the range of choices offered or by making the options more complex.

- Depending on your goals, leave room for students to change their minds if they are disappointed with a choice they have made. If time and management require the student to make a choice and stick with it, make this clear when you present the available options.

- As students become more capable, encourage students to participate in setting up choices whenever possible. Clear limits are especially important in such cases; suggest that they present their options to you for a final OK before they act.

- If students suggest a choice that you think is inappropriate, tell them your concerns and ask if they can come up with a different choice. If something is simply non-negotiable, say so, but also try to present other options within those limits.

# 14 Maintaining positive behaviors

I n the past, many teacher education programs that addressed discipline issues have focused on using praise as positive reinforcement for cooperative behavior. This emphasis probably grew out of the intention to discourage negative teacher behaviors, such as yelling and criticizing. Unfortunately, the situations that provoke teachers to yell and criticize generally are not conducive to using positive reinforcement effectively.

I became aware of the frequent misunderstanding and misapplication of this technique when I began observing beginning teachers in their classrooms. One year during the first week of school, I walked into a classroom to see Ms. Harding standing in front of the room, trying to get her 25 first-graders settled down so she could continue with the lesson. Despite her firm and patient requests, the students were out of their seats, yelling, playing on the rug, fighting over toys, or running through the language center. Ms. Harding began to feel the panic of being out of control, and frantically thought over the tricks she had learned in student teaching. She managed to focus on the one student who was still (thankfully) in his seat.

*I like the way Bobby is sitting,* she announced.

With that, Bobby perked up and sat at attention, beaming. Although one or two other students did stop to look at Bobby, the chaos continued.

Ms. Harding tried again. *I really like the way Bobby is sitting.*

Bobby sat up even straighter, folded his hands, and smiled proudly. Again, the rest of the class was barely distracted from their fun. And as Ms. Harding continued, louder and more intense in her praise for Bobby, his behavior got better and better while the rest of the class continued to fall apart. Ms. Harding was literally saved by the lunch bell, which got the students' attention long enough for her to furiously proclaim that unless they all took their seats that instant, they would never leave that room again!

So much for positive reinforcement, she thought. Too bad. Because positive reinforcement does work (remember the dancing pigeons of Ed Psych 101?). The technique is logical and well-founded. Why, then, does it seem to lose so much in its transfer to human beings in a classroom?

Part of the problem seems to be in the use of the reinforcer, which, in broad terms, can be described as a device— whether word, object, or deed—that increases the likelihood of the student repeating or continuing a particular behavior. In order for a reinforcer to work, it must immediately follow the desired behavior. (The student has to somehow initiate the behavior.) In other words, we cannot reinforce a student's handwriting if he has not written anything and we cannot reinforce her quiet behavior if she will not clam up.

Positive reinforcement encourages the student to continue or repeat a particular behavior. Frustration and disillusionment with the technique can occur when teachers attempt to use reinforcement to evoke a desired behavior. Ms. Harding discovered this problem when she found that the reinforcer (her praise) had a positive effect only on the student she reinforced. Praising Bobby was not effective in getting the other students to settle down and imitate him. True, on occasion praising Bobby might get Susie to sit down. And while this might satisfy a teacher's immediate objectives, let's take a look at how this process works and what it can cost.

Positive feedback can come in the form of a high grade; a sticker on a paper; a positive comment written in a margin;

an activity or privilege; or a nod, smile, wink, or touch from the teacher. As long as it follows the cooperative behavior and is meaningful to the student, it works as a reinforcer. Now certain reinforcers, such as praise, are more likely than others to communicate teacher approval. When these reinforcers work, they do so because they appeal to a basic human need to feel valued and worthwhile. Since many of our students value our approval, and since praise is such a familiar motivator, we are often tempted to use it as a reinforcer. Although usually delivered with sincere intentions, praise does have its price.

When Ms. Harding said, *I like the way Bobby is sitting*, she was delivering a judgment: Bobby's sitting was good and teacher-pleasing; the behavior of the rest of the class, clearly, was not. By praising Bobby, she was communicating *If you act like him, you too will be good and please the teacher.* (This is not to say that we should not acknowledge our preferences to our students. In fact, it would be difficult to mask what pleases us and what does not.) But such deliberate praise tends to overemphasize the pleasure we take in our students' cooperation. Using the phrase *I like . . .* as a judgment of a student's behavior encourages the student to be good simply to make us happy and implies a lack of worth and acceptance when he or she does not.

> **Using *I like* encourages the student to be good simply to make us happy.**

Sound familiar? Welcome back to encouraging obedience and pleasing the teacher. Sure Susie will sit down when I praise Bobby: she wants me to like her too. It sounds efficient, but such judgments can build dependence on external approval for self-esteem, as well as interfere with the development of internally motivated, responsible behavior. Had Ms. Harding wanted to reinforce Bobby's behavior—for Bobby's sake—she could have simply recognized how quickly he got quiet or even the fact that he was ready. And she could have done it very quietly. The fact that she announced her approval of one student to the rest of the class is a good indication of her desire to manipulate the behavior of the other students.

Praise has other drawbacks. When we praise someone to try to evoke performance or cooperation from others, the negative implications are obvious, especially to the others. In this case, praise of Bobby is criticism of everyone else. This reaction is especially common if an unrelated event or situation is praised: *Your brother was such a good student* or *But your other papers were so neat.* Announcing to the class that *José wrote the best story in the class.* simply informs other students that they are not quite up to José's talents. (Do we really want everybody to write like José, even if his writing is great?) This tendency to reinforce and promote uniformity is another holdover from industrial-age thinking. Such attempts at manipulation promote win-lose competitiveness and *I can't* attitudes.

Even among the students receiving praise, the technique can create problems. For one thing, praise reinforces a dependence on someone else for feelings of self-worth. (After a while, even the absence of praise can be perceived as criticism.)

Second, not all students are comfortable being singled out. Our approval is only effective as long as it is important to our students. However, the need for approval often competes with the students' need for peer approval or with the students' need for personal satisfaction (doing it anyway). Sometimes even cooperative students, feeling pressured or embarrassed, respond to praise with disruption or withdrawal.

Often implicit in praise is the expectation that once demonstrated, there is no reason for the behavior to diminish or discontinue. This expectation is communicated subtly (*See, I knew you could do it!*), directly (*Why can't all your papers look this good?*), or even sarcastically (*Well, it's about time!*). If our praise even remotely suggests *and you'd better keep it up.* It may actually produce the opposite effect.

Children can be extremely sensitive to our motives, even when we are not clear about them ourselves. Even very young children can detect insincerity and manipulation. One kindergarten teacher told of how a boy crumpled up a paper she had just gushed over. *She just says that to get you to be good,* she heard him tell his friend.

If we tell Johnny that he is smart, for example, in order to get him to act it, he will see right through the statement. Such flattery does not build self-esteem, regardless of the sincerity of our intentions. A student who does not feel smart will certainly hear our praise with suspicion, believing either that we just do not understand or that we must not be so smart ourselves. That student might attempt to prove through games that we do not know what we are talking about. Our endeavors will be successful at eroding trust more than anything else.

The fact that verbal reinforcement sounds positive has led many teachers to believe that this type of statement holds the key to a student's self-concept. True, hearing nice things or statements of approval does feel good (if the person communicating those feelings means anything at all to us). But self-esteem does not mean *I am great because my teacher thinks I am great.*

Self-esteem is a by-product of empowerment and requires a sense of control in one's life. If we are offering opportunities for the student to make choices and experience the positive outcomes of his choosing, we are building self-esteem. If we are providing a success-oriented structure in which the student can achieve, we are building self-esteem. The operant word is *self*: if a genuine sense of worth does not come from the student's self, positive external messages will be superficial and fragile at best.

Despite all these cautions, positive verbal reinforcement can be a legitimate and highly effective tool in a 21st century classroom. In addition to strengthening desirable student behavior, reinforcing statements allow us to focus on the positive, communicate respect for the child's efforts and personal needs, help the child develop internalized management and motivational capabilities, and encourage an *I can* attitude. But like any teaching technique, it can be set up to either maintain internally motivated, responsible behavior, or obedience and teacher-dependence.

The last two chapters talked about using choices and contingencies to elicit or motivate desired behaviors. Positive reinforcement is what we rely on once those behaviors occur. The motivators (contingencies) that encourage the cooperative behavior become the reinforcers (positive outcomes) once the cooperative behavior occurs. In other words, the possibility to run an errand may have motivated Billy to do his work; once the work was done, the actual privilege reinforced his cooperation. This reinforcement, so long as it is need-fulfilling and available within a reasonable amount of time after the performance of the desirable behavior, increases the probability that the behavior will recur.

**The first step in the process is recognizing the behavior.**

Even in cases in which the student has access to a tangible reward or privilege, verbal reinforcement can provide additional support—at the completion of the task or even along the way—emphasizing the value of the positive behavior as well as the connection between cooperation and payoff. But we will often encounter other student successes—a breakthrough in learning, an unanticipated contribution, or the sudden appearance of a new behavior for which no contingency had been previously specified. The immediacy of verbal reinforcement can be especially effective in these cases.

The first step in the process is recognizing the behavior. Recognition sounds like praise, but there are significant differences between the two. For one thing, praise tends to be stated in general terms (*You were good today.*) while recognition tends to be more specific (*You put all the art materials away before you left the center.*) Recognition is also more descriptive and less judgmental than praise. For example, instead of stating *I like the way you remembered your library book.* say, *I see you remembered your library book. Look at how neat your handwriting has become!* is preferable to *I like the way your handwriting has improved.* Recognition is expressed with enthusiasm and excitement, but it does not carry the weight of the teacher's needs, values, or judgments.

When recognition uses valuing words, the value is connected to the performance or achievement, not the person: *The ending to the story was really exciting.* or *You're making great progress in spelling.* Recognition can also express appreciation: *You really added a lot to our discussion. Nice try.*, or *My, you really worked hard today!* or even short, non-descriptive comments like *Great!* or *I agree.* But the appreciation is not expressed as a benefit to the teacher. While this may sound somewhat impersonal, recognition has its own power without connecting the student's worth (or ability to please) to the student's behavior. Recognition validates behavior without making a judgment.

**The next step involves verbally connecting the performance to the positive outcome.**

From this perspective, we can even get away with an occasional outburst of praise, provided that our sentiments are genuine, spontaneous, and not designed to influence or manipulate. In a non-conflict setting, such feelings can communicate a great deal of respect and appreciation for a student and his or her achievement, particularly in a high-trust, win-win environment.

Once we have acknowledged the behavior we wish to reinforce, the next step involves verbally connecting the performance or cooperation to the positive outcome. Here again, however, we should be aware of the difference between our needs and those of the students. Often our own needs are tied up in the request we make. We want our students to write neatly so that we will be able to read their work or to put the materials away so that we will not have to. If students cooperate because of what's in it for us, they are being teacher-pleasers. When we reinforce their cooperation by linking it to how it pays off for us—even if their cooperation is self-motivated—we reinforce obedience and undermine their internal motivation.

What we really want to reinforce is the connection between the students' behavior and what's in it for them: *You put all your materials away. Now you can go to lunch.* This second sentence, *Now you can go to lunch.* goes beyond simply acknowledging the behavior. Adding this step verbally reinforces the personal empowerment in being able to positively self-manage. Restating what is in it for them after they have completed a behavior strengthens personal responsibility.

As with contingencies and rewards, it's easy to trip over personal values, project what is important to us, and make assumptions about the students' values. As innocent as they may seem, statements such as *You must be proud.* or *I'll bet you're happy now.* actually tell students how we think they should feel. Even if the students have suggested to us that they will indeed be proud or happy when they have achieved some goal, we can simply ask them how they feel and support their accomplishment by tying it in with something concrete: *Now you can go on to the next level.*

We also need to be careful that we do not connect students' positive behavior to something they perceive as negative. (How would you feel if I recognized the great job you did cleaning my bathroom by saying, *Now that you're finished, you can iron?*) In order for our statements to actually reinforce, they must have meaning and make sense to students. Connections that promise *Now people will think you're neat* or *Now you can help grade papers* may not be punitive, but a child who does not need to be perceived as neat or one who has no interest in grading papers will probably shrug in response. *That will help you get into the college of your choice* will only be meaningful to a kid who is striving for that goal.

The best verbal reinforcers are those tied to the actual (or realistically possible) experiences of our students. For example, consider the following comment: *You remembered to put the caps back on the markers. Now they won't be dried out when you want to use them tomorrow.* This statement will have a greater impact on a child who has actually tried to write with a dried-out marker than one who never has. Still, the reinforcer maintains its validity in the fact that it is directly connected to the benefits to the student; even if the student cannot imagine the negative consequences, we are still reinforcing the cause-and-effect nature of his or her behavior.

If the positive outcome of a student's behavior is too remote or abstract, we can reinforce the behavior by connecting it to something more immediate and concrete, as we did in setting up contingencies. For example, learning to regroup in addition problems has a number of positive outcomes, but most of them are related to being able to do

**The best verbal reinforcers are those tied to the actual experiences of our students.**

something more complex at some point in the future. When a child experiences a breakthrough in this process, it may be quite reassuring to tell him that now he will have an easier time with the next lesson; but we will probably achieve a more powerful effect by stating, *Now that you understand this skill, you can work with these new math puzzles and games.* The purpose of reinforcement is to maintain the desired behavior. Even if we occasionally need to tie the behavior to an outcome that is not directly related to the task itself (*Since you finished and corrected your work early today, you can take this note around to the other teachers if you like.*), we are still increasing the likelihood that the desired behavior will recur, as long as the outcome is meaningful.

The following chart presents guidelines to use in developing effective recognition and reinforcement.

**The purpose of reinforcement is to maintain the desired behavior.**

# Guidelines for Recognition/Reinforcement.

- Use positive reinforcement—verbal or non-verbal—to acknowledge and strengthen already-existing behaviors. [1]

- Watch for a tendency to use praise to help a student solve a problem or feel good about himself or herself. Such messages will be superficial at best, and will not contribute to the student's genuine sense of self worth.

- Avoid using teacher approval as a means of reinforcing desired behavior. Learn to distinguish between reinforcers intended to maintain a particular student behavior and genuine expressions of appreciation, affection, or enjoyment of your students. In a win-win classroom, behaviors such as a smile, touch, nod, or wink—which obviously communicate the fact that the teacher is pleased—are not used as expressions of conditional approval or caring. Although they may sometimes be used as reinforcers, such behaviors may also appear randomly, regardless of the student's performance or behavior, as expressions of appreciation or affection.

- Phrase your reinforcements as an affirmation or acknowledgment of a behavior the student has demonstrated and the positive consequences now available (not as *If . . . then . . .* statements). Reinforcements may be effectively communicated in either oral or written form.

- To reinforce a desirable behavior (in oral or written form), first describe the behavior that took place. Be specific and concrete and avoid making judgments about the behavior or the worth of the student.

- Look for the positive. You can almost always find something good to recognize in any performance. Reinforce what was done right and work on the rest.

- Whenever possible, attach a comment that connects the immediate benefits of the student's behavior to the behavior itself. (Occasionally, it may be appropriate to state the positive outcomes in terms of their benefits to the group.) Focus on what is in it for the student, making sure the outcome is positive and meaningful. Avoid projecting your own feelings and values, which may or may not be relevant to those of the student, or suggesting how the student should feel.

- Perhaps because of the rigidity of roles during the factory era, there was a tendency for teachers to recognize certain behaviors in boys (such as strength, mechanical skill, and ability in math and the sciences) more frequently than in girls (who were more often reinforced for neatness, attractiveness, and writing and artistic abilities). In recognizing students, be aware of any tendencies to promote stereotypes.

[1] Use other strategies to encourage the student to initiate a desired behavior or to discourage a disruptive behavior.

On a separate sheet of paper draw three columns. In column **Exercise**
one, identify five specific desired behaviors—that is, behaviors you want your students to exhibit.

In column two, imagine that a student has just demonstrated
one of the desired behaviors you identified in column one.
Write a recognition statement you might use to acknowledge
the student's cooperation.

In column three, write a statement that connects the student's cooperation to a positive outcome (what's in it for the
student).

| Desired behavior | Recognition statement | What's in it for the student |
|---|---|---|
|  |  |  |

Tell which positive student behaviors you have recognized (once the behaviors were demonstrated) during the past two or three days [2]:

How specific were your recognition statements in describing the desired behavior?

How successful were you in avoiding communicating personal judgments and teacher approval?

How successful were you in avoiding attempts to use praise of one student to elicit a cooperative behavior from another?

How successful were you in avoiding attempts to use praise to dismiss a student's problem or make him feel better?

Describe some of the instances in which you were able to connect the student's behavior to its positive outcomes.

How well were you able to focus on the immediate benefits to the student?

In what ways are you satisfied with the reinforcement strategies you currently use?

In what ways would you like to change or expand these strategies?

2 You may want to tape-record a lesson or ask a colleague to observe. In either case, the object of this activity is to identify specific language: what you say to recognize positive behavior and also how you connect it to the positive consequences to the student.

# 15 Encouraging independence and problem-solving

How many times in the course of your day do you find a student at your elbow with some problem or other: *What are we supposed to do?*

*My dog ate my homework.*

*I can't find the paste.*

*Alex is bothering me.*

Our students' lives seem cluttered at times with problems that, they will try to convince us, require our help. These interactions can be rather distracting: they eat up a lot of valuable instructional time even though they usually can be resolved without our intervention. Yet students have a number of reasons for wanting to share their problems with us.

Sometimes students share just for the sake of sharing and the social contact and conversation the interaction can offer. The student may not even be seeking solutions as much as acknowledgment and validation. But sharing problems through whining or complaining can also be seen as a way of dumping responsibility for something students do not want to resolve, although frequently students— especially good "order-takers"—honestly feel incapable or powerless in facing even the simplest dilemma. It is often a good way to get our attention or provoke a time-killing response.

A student experiencing a crisis does need our help. Furthermore, there are certain traumas, such as abuse, neglect, divorce, or death, which probably require more support than a classroom teacher is able to provide. Clearly, these instances should be referred for outside intervention, although our support and understanding can be very reassuring in the meantime [1].

Fortunately, most of the crises affecting our students on a day-to-day basis are more like *She looked at me!* or *Somebody stole my pencil.* When a student brings problems to the classroom and is unable or unwilling to solve it on his or her own, it can very quickly become our problem. For our mental health and the needs of the other students, we should try to prevent student problems from interfering with our needs. But how do we put the responsibility for a problem back on his or her shoulders—without abandoning the person—when these problems do come up?

Teacher-dependence and the need for attention can become a never-ending distraction. Even our deepest needs to be needed can be sapped by the constancy of a train of students pulling on our sleeves. Mr. Marshall, a teacher in a multi-age (grades 1 - 3) classroom, was plagued by one student he privately dubbed Shadow. No matter where Mr. Marshall went—in or out of the classroom—it seemed that Shadow was never far behind. Shadow didn't need much time; he was just always there. One day, Mr. Marshall decided to keep a tab on the number of times Shadow *needed* him; by lunchtime it was nearly forty-eight!

Now, while the student's need for attention is certainly the student's problem, his inability to meet that need without making his teacher crazy invites joint ownership of the problem. Had Mr. Marshall been exclusively concerned with his own needs, he might have been able to *win* by isolating the student in some way. Had his concerns been only for the student's needs, Mr. Marshall could have completely abandoned his own need for privacy and time with other students to devote his attention to Shadow. But Mr. Marshall came up with a win-win solution that not only acknowledged the student's need for his time, help, and attention, but also set limits that would protect his own needs. (He also contacted Shadow's parents to discuss his intentions.)

He approached Shadow with five paper clips and a plan: *I understand that you need to talk to me during the day and I really enjoy visiting with you. But you know, sometimes I spend so much time with you that I don't get to talk to the other students and I don't get my work done. What I'd like to do is to give you these five paper clips. Put them on your belt, OK?*

*Now whenever you want to talk to me, it'll cost you one paper clip. These need to last until recess; I'll give you five more afterwards until lunch. As long as you have a paper clip, I'll be happy to take the time out to talk to you. Once they're gone, you'll have to wait until after recess to get some more.*

Of course, on the first go-round, it didn't take too long for the paper clips to disappear; Mr. Marshall knew it would be a very long time until recess came, and that his consistency during that stretch was essential. Being out of paper clips didn't slow Shadow down a bit, but Mr. Marshall's reaction did.

On the first five visits, Mr. Marshall asked for a paper clip and then gave his full attention to Shadow. On the sixth visit Mr. Marshall said, *I'm sorry, I can't see you now. Let's talk at recess.* He then turned around and continued with what he had been doing. If Shadow persisted, so did Mr. Marshall. Firmly. Politely. Never once did he give Shadow the impression that he was angry or did not care; this was not a moral victory—but simply a matter of everyone's rights being protected.

> A rule of thumb for problem-solving in the classroom: the person with the problem is responsible for its solution.

Suddenly Shadow had to determine the importance of his questions and if Mr. Marshall was the only person who could help him. He was somewhat more selective with his use of the five late-morning paper clips, even more so by the end of the day. By the third day, he was down from 20 to 10 clips a day; by the third week, he had been weaned from the paper clips—and his need for Mr. Marshall's constant attention—completely. By that point, he had learned to work with other students and was much more capable of solving real problems on his own. He became more aware of Mr. Marshall's needs, as well as the other students' needs for attention, and made genuine attempts to avoid interrupting. Not bad for a six-year-old.

A rule of thumb for problem-solving in the classroom (or anywhere): the person with the problem is responsible for the solution of the problem without making it anyone else's problem. Yet, regardless of our commitment to these goals, it is still easy to get hooked by our students' needs, even when we are *not* really needed.

Behind this temptation is a belief rooted in factory-era authority relationships that suggests a leader should be aware of and involved in every aspect of the group's functioning in order to maintain control. The 21st century classroom emphasizes student self-control. Students are encouraged to take the initiative for solving their problems within the limits of classroom rules. There *are* times we need to jump in, but for the most part, we do not need to know that the problem exists!

Another temptation comes from the fact that it is usually very easy for us to see how the problem could be resolved or avoided. Sometimes this feeling comes from the frustration of being interrupted (if we just solve this problem for them, maybe it will go away). Sometimes it comes from a lack of trust in our students' problem-solving capabilities (which may come from win-lose programming).

If we view one of our roles as that of *rescuer*, we are also likely to believe solving other people's problems is part of the job. Many of our students have sold us on their helplessness. Assuming responsibility for their problems can be especially tempting if we are inclined to protect them. Add to that our needs to be wanted, important, wise, and in charge, and it is easy to understand the difficulty involved in separating ourselves from our students' needs.

**Every time we solve a problem for our students, we rob them of a chance to practice responsibility and interfere with their learning and growth.**

Falling into this trap, however, does no one any favors in the long run. To begin with, every time we solve a problem that our students can solve themselves, we rob them of a chance to practice responsibility and actually interfere with the students' learning and growth. It may appear that we are saving time, but we are instead creating opportunities for future interruptions to occur because we are reinforcing helplessness and teacher-dependence. And it won't take long before we start feeling resentful and reacting negatively.

Most of the time, our students' problems compete with our own needs for privacy, concentration, and our ability to stay on task. After a while, the interruptions and lack of self-management are bound to get on our nerves. Whether it is the nature of the problem or the teacher-dependence itself, when our patience wears thin, our reaction is not likely to be very helpful or supportive.

Let's face it—some of their problems can seem strange or even silly to us. Once a student approached me on the verge of hysteria, claiming that one of the other students had called her a camel. Sometimes trying to take these incidents seriously can be a challenge, but it is important to remember that the pain and stress the student is experiencing is very real. It may help if we pause to regain our patience and perspective before we say something that would dismiss or trivialize their feelings: *Don't be ridiculous. You can't possibly be upset about that!* Sarcasm and distractions are no more effective: *Why aren't you this worried about your math grades?* These kinds of comments are problematic because they judge what students are feeling as wrong or unimportant, and tell students how they should feel. The message will either result in frustration and resentment on the part of the student (which can erode trust in teacher-student relationships), or self-doubt and eventual repression (which can have serious long-term negative effects for the student). Denying the problem, ignoring the student, or refusing to listen can be just as invalidating and nonproductive.

Overreacting, or reacting with anger, can also be damaging: *I guess I'm just going to have to move you if you can't get along with anyone. If you weren't so irresponsible, you wouldn't be having these problems.* or *That does it! I'm calling your parents.* Now the student has two problems: not only is the original issue unresolved, but somehow she is being scolded, punished, or made to feel wrong for having the problem in the first place!

Another ineffective way of handling student problems is by reacting with advice (telling the student how to solve the problem). As innocent and effective as it may seem, there are two major drawbacks to giving advice. For one thing, advising immediately draws us into the problem, making us responsible for it and its solution. (Our advice also makes us vulnerable to blame if we are wrong.) Second, giving advice not only deprives the student of the opportunity to learn responsibility and problem-solving techniques, it also suggests that she is incapable (often heard as *too dumb*) of doing so.

Closely related is the tendency to ask a student *why*: why he does not have his homework, why he forgot his pencil, or why Lamont was bothering him. Asking why is a common reaction that seems harmless, but it also engages us in the problem and invites excuses, implying that if the student is creative—or pathetic enough—he can get out of his responsibility. Excuses invite the arbitrary use of teacher power *(Impress me and maybe I'll let you out of it)* and more often than not evoke negative reactions, such as criticisms, lectures, or punishment. Excuses also invite us to solve the problem for the student. Does it really matter if Alfred does not have his homework because a tornado took it out of his lunchbox or because he felt like watching TV instead? Does he no longer need to turn it in? (Setting a blanket *grace period* or offering almost full credit for work handed in a day late can accommodate students with more serious excuses as well as those who have simply made poor choices.)

If the student is indeed going through a crisis that is interfering with her school life, the issue will involve more than one missing homework assignment and will probably not come out in the form of an excuse. True, a number of similar incidents may point to something more serious; however, asking for excuses about one situation is not the most direct route to the heart of a real problem. When something more serious is wrong, it is far more likely that the student, a parent, support staff member, administrator, or outside agent will approach us in an entirely different manner.

**We need to let students know that there will be times that we will not be able to help them with their problems.**

Success-oriented problem-solving requires some groundwork. To begin, we need to let students know—from the start—that there will be times we will not be able to help them with their problems, and that our insistence on their finding their own solutions does not mean that we do not care. We also need to remind them that solving their problems must not create problems for anyone else. I win-You win, remember?

In addition, we need to be sure that there are options available within these limits by which the students can indeed resolve their conflicts on their own. For example, if a student is upset that another student is bothering her or interfering with her ability to do her work, is the student allowed to move her desk or find another place to work? If the student does not have necessary materials, does he have the option of asking around before class starts to borrow a pencil or share a book? Without positive options, students will surely find negative routes.

And the better we can express limits before we are invited to help out, the more consistently we can enforce them. For example, take a simple statement such as *Open your books to page 35*. Regardless of the age of the students, the size of the group, or the location of the school, there seems to be a universal and immediate student response: *What page?* Most of us become exasperated at having to explain everything more than once. (Every time we do, no matter how angry and frustrated we are, we tell the students that it is OK for them to not listen the first time.)

Yet there are success-oriented ways to discourage this type of teacher-dependence. For one thing, make sure you have everyone's attention before you start. (A second-grade teacher asks her students to *Look at me* whenever she has anything important for the group to hear. More importantly, she waits until all activity and talking cease and all eyes are on her before she explains.) Next, tell the students before you give your directions: *I will only say this once.* Finally, provide positive options for students who may be tired or inattentive, or those who have difficulty remembering or understanding oral directions. Writing the directions on the board or allowing students to go to one another for help (without disturbing anyone) make it much easier for students to become independent and self-managing.

Tattling is another behavior that can drive anyone to distraction. I don't mean reports of a fire in the library or a stranger in the bathroom. (You can be sure that no matter how strict your no-tattling rules are, you will hear about the serious stuff.) I am talking about the annoying attempts to drag us into peer conflicts that are not life-threatening: *Nicole was looking at me. Garry said a bad word. Alvin kicked my chair.* What do we do when we have set everything up to encourage student self-management only to find a child tapping on our shoulder because somebody called her a camel? What happens if we refuse to allow these problems to become our own?

One third-grade teacher told her students that she had simply gotten too busy to listen to them tattling. *I know you want to tell me these things and I don't want you to think I'm not interested. I'm sorry that they happen, but I can't help right now!* [2] She also made herself available at a later time to talk over the problem and the student's attempts to solve it. By assuring students that she was truly concerned, yet unwilling to become directly involved in their conflicts, she put the responsibility back on the kids. And by providing some outlets that did not create additional problems, she made it possible for students to choose positive alternatives to negative situations. Finally, she not only avoided attempts to draw her into problems she did not own, but she also reinforced the students' sense of their own abilities to resolve conflicts and fulfill their needs.

Another teacher, totally frustrated with an endless stream of tattling sixth graders, finally exploded, *From here on in, the only time you are allowed to tattle is if somebody dies!* The students got the point, had a laugh, and still, on occasion, forgot the rule. However, from then on, any time a student came up to complain about another student, all the teacher had to do was remind the complainer that since the other student was still alive, the two of them had to work out the problem peacefully between themselves.

Another way to avoid owning student problems is by removing the power and morality from conflicts. For example, many teachers, especially those working with upper-grade students or in departmentalized settings, frequently complain about the times their kids show up unprepared. If a student shows up in our classroom without a pencil or a book, obviously he or she has a problem. But the student's lack of preparation does not automatically have to become our problem.

Something as simple as not having a pencil can become a moral issue: *But they need a pencil. They know they need a pencil. They should have a pencil. And yet here they are empty-handed. What's wrong with them?*

In a win-lose classroom, teachers typically blow up, criticize, and deliver a lecture about responsibility and self-sufficiency, after which they either give out a pencil or they do not. But in the meantime, they have killed at least a minute or two of instructional time. They have gotten upset and, as a result, their students are not any more self-managing or responsible. Even if they have taught the kids to come prepared tomorrow to keep teacher from getting upset, their cooperation is still not self-motivated.

It is possible to deal with a forgotten pencil in a non-emotional, disengaged, non-judgmental frame of mind. We handle similar crises with adults in that manner all the time. (Have you ever forgotten your pen as you went to write a check in the supermarket? How did you solve the problem? How would you have felt if the cashier had yelled at you about being irresponsible? After all, you knew you were going shopping. You knew you would have to pay for those groceries, didn't you? See?)

Neither do we need to take on a student's lack of preparedness as our own problem—or as a personal assault. What are your rules? What are your resources? Do you have enough pencils to keep a few on hand? Are you willing to loan them out without making a production out of it? If not, say so: *Sorry, I can't help you.*

The real issue is that the student needs something to write with in order to do her work, right? Sure it would be nice if she remembered, but for the moment, she did not. It usually does not cost much to loan a kid a pencil or keep a few in a can for emergencies. It certainly does not cost anything to give a student a minute to find a pencil while we get the class ready or after everyone begins seatwork. This is the heart of success orientation and win-win. (I always found that the less fuss I made over pencils, the fewer problems my kids had remembering. And when my extras disappeared, they borrowed from one another.) Although the habits from a win-lose perspective would have us believe otherwise, a forgotten pencil does not devalue a student. Loaning him a pencil no more teaches a child to be irresponsible than your need to borrow one at the check-out counter will ensure future forgetfulness.

When a student has a problem, we can provide support without actually becoming responsible for the problem. Sometimes just listening is enough, although listening in conjunction with nodding and encouraging comments (*Uh-huh, I see,* or *Tell me more*) can be even more effective. Very often, just having the chance to unload can help the student process the various dimensions of the problem well enough to see a solution.

Often, the less we say, the more helpful we can be. When we are able to listen—without jumping in to advise, ask questions, or share our own experiences—we show appreciation for his or her concerns and still leave full responsibility with the child. By not telling a student what to do, we are also demonstrating our trust in him or her.

**Acknowledging the student's concerns, validating her feelings, yet leaving responsibility for the solution of a problem with the student, is support in the truest, kindest, and most helpful sense of the word.**

More elaborate responses are also appropriate. For example, Active Listening [3] is a valuable feedback process in which the listener communicates his or her understanding of the speaker's message by restating what the speaker has said in the listener's own words, without evaluating, judging, interpreting or commiserating. This tool can help the student gain further understanding of the problem and find his own way out. And as we develop our ability to objectively reflect what we are hearing, we can also avoid the more familiar negative responses.

So, when one of your students complains that somebody called her a camel, instead of questioning (*What does that mean?*), minimizing (*Why does that bother you?*), advising (*Just ignore him.*), threatening (*If you don't stop coming up here . . .*), or blaming (*What did you do to him?*), we can simply restate the heart of what the student is telling us: *It upsets you when someone calls you a name.*

Sometimes this response is enough: you have acknowledged the student's concern, validated her feelings, and let her know you understood what she was saying to you. You have also left the responsibility for the solution of the problem with the student because your response did not involve you in the cause or solution of the problem. This is support in the truest, kindest, and most helpful sense of the word.

Regardless of your response to a student's complaint, if she is new to solving her own problems (or insecure about her ability to do so), it is likely that she came to you in the first place in the hopes of having you fix the situation. Even if you have set the stage for personal responsibility ahead of time, your refusal to get involved can add to the student's frustration. If you have time to talk it out then and there and are willing to do so, fine. But more often than not, you will be in the middle of something, unable to help the student work through the process. In these instances, reassure the student that she is not being abandoned (*Let's talk about it some more at lunchtime*) and continue with your work.

At times, we may need to work with individuals or groups of students on a variety of responsible behaviors, including positive social interactions, conflict resolution, and alternatives to blaming and making excuses. In addition to instructional activities (such as values clarification or role-playing), specific problems may be addressed with additional dialogue. If we choose to *talk it out* with students, it may be best to do so in a more private, non-conflict setting.

**Setting limits protects the teacher, other students, pets, plants . . . yet leaves the student options for solving problems and getting his or her needs met.**

Still, we should probably be doing more listening than talking. Your role moves from problem-solver/rescuer to encourager/facilitator. Instead of asking questions aimed at blaming or advising, we can encourage students to talk about, process, and resolve problems with certain questions stated in a warm and receptive tone. The questions can focus on their goals and needs (*What do you want? What are you trying to accomplish? What would make you happy?*); their plans (*What can you do to get what you want? What's your plan?*); probable outcomes (*What do you suppose will happen if you do that? Will that get you what you want? Is there any way it might hurt you later?*); and alternatives (*What else can you do? What if that doesn't work?*).

Note that there is a difference between setting limits and giving advice that has to do primarily with problem ownership. Both are forms of *telling the student what to do*. Advice is usually directed to the student's problem; setting limits is useful when the teacher has a problem. When Mr. Marshall gave Shadow the paper clips, he was not telling the student how to resolve his need for the teacher's attention. Instead, Mr. Marshall was taking care of his own problem—his need to limit the number of times Shadow could ask for help. Setting limits protects the teacher, other students, pets, plants, and classroom furnishings; it still leaves the student options for solving problems and getting his or her needs met.

Even our willingness to sit and listen has limits. Students often need to talk when it is not convenient for us. So we try to assess the urgency of the student's needs, asking, *Is it important?* Of course the student will think so. What we are really asking is for the student to determine, *Will I think it's more important than what I'm doing at the moment?* If the student is in the throes of a very serious trauma or physical distress that requires immediate attention, we will not need to ask.

The rest of the time we can, instead, affirm the student's need for attention as well as our willingness to give (they win) as soon as we are free (we win). If you are not in the mood to listen or your patience is questionable, your tone of voice and body language will make that clear. Be honest: *I am too busy (tired, angry) right now to give you the kind of time and attention you deserve.* Then give the student a specific time to return: *I do want to talk to you. I'll be finished with this group in ten minutes. Let's talk then.*

Occasionally a student will get extremely upset over a seemingly insignificant comment or event. Because a hysterical child can be disruptive and annoying, our immediate impulse is just to get him to settle down. Angry, negative responses *(Oh, stop it! You're acting like a baby!)* are not only insensitive, invalidating, and repressive, they are not very likely to calm the student down.

Feelings are neither right nor wrong. Whether or not we would react as our student has, her feelings are real. Especially when a student is upset, we are most caring and helpful when we can communicate acceptance of the student and her feelings. Still, this does not mean we need to make the student's problem—or her feelings—our own, nor does it suggest we have to try to carry on a conversation with a student who is gasping for air between sobs. But it does allow us to provide support (an understanding word, a reassuring touch, an invitation to go get a drink or be by herself, and an unlimited supply of tissues) while we wait for the child to settle down a bit. *Let's talk as soon as you calm down* tells the child it is OK to feel whatever she is feeling, that we will give her time and space, and, at the same time, limit our dealings with hysteria. Upset or not, the child is accepted and valued. And in this environment, the student is safe to risk the learning that is involved in becoming an independent problem-solver.

[1] Kendall Johnson's book, *Classroom Crisis* (Turnpoint Publishing, Claremont, CA, 1987) provides some outstanding guidelines for helping students deal with crises and traumatic events in their lives.

[2] Johnson presented her students with the option of *putting it in writing*, supplying a form that asked the following: Your name; The name of the person who is bothering you; Something nice about that person; The problem; What you are going to do about the problem.

[3] Thomas Gordon's books: *Teacher-Effectiveness-Training, Parent-Effectiveness-Training, and Leader-Effectiveness-Training*), offer a more elaborate description of Active Listening and some excellent examples of the process, along with suggestions for its use.

When a problem occurs in the classroom, it is always best if **Activity** we can evaluate the situation before acting—or reacting. To practice, think of a problem one of your students recently asked you to share or solve. (Keep this list of questions at hand to plan, practice, and evaluate other incidents as they come up.)

Describe the problem below:

In what way could this be (or become) your problem?

What do you need to do to *prevent* it from becoming your problem?

What do you need to do to *keep* it from becoming your problem?

In what ways have you *set the stage* for your students to solve this problem (and others) on their own?

What else might you do to avoid similar future incidents?

What options does the student have for solving this problem on his or her own?

What other options might you make available for similar future incidents?

In what way have you acknowledged the student's needs and feelings?

How did you help the student solve this problem without making it your own?

How successful were you at avoiding a negative response (advising, asking why, criticizing, scolding, moralizing, trivializing, and so forth)?

Which negative responses are most difficult for you to avoid?

In what ways have your students shown growth in independence and problem-solving skills?

In what ways have you become better able to separate yourself from your students' problems (and turn the responsibility back over to them)?

What are your plans to further enhance your growth and theirs in this area?

# 16    Structuring consequences

Up to this point, this book has been devoted to the prevention of problems and negative behaviors. Unfortunately, we can devote our entire teaching existence to developing positive interactions and win-win dynamics and still, on occasion, encounter and have to deal with disruptions. Even with the best intentions to separate ourselves from conflicts, students may lack the skills for resolving their problems nondisruptively. The disturbance can quickly become problematic for us and the rest of the class and, on occasion, even other classes. Negative behavior can occur in any classroom; however, these incidents are handled quite differently in a 21st century environment than in the autocratic classroom of past decades.

For example, imagine that Carlos and William are fighting over who gets to read a particular book first. Both are pulling on the book and shouting at one another, creating quite an uproar in the classroom. Students are being distracted from their work, the teacher is unable to continue the lesson, and Heaven knows what's happening to the book.

There are a number of possible teacher responses to this conflict behavior. For example, a teacher might get up and burst out, *What's wrong with you two? Put that book down and get to your seats! You'll both be in after school to write a few pages on how you are supposed to behave in class.* Other than restoring quiet, the only real benefit of this win-lose technique is that it *might* protect the book. This is a punitive response. It teaches more about the teacher's power than about effective ways to share books or resolve conflicts. The teacher has taken responsibility for the misbehavior; the students have learned nothing about negotiating or problem-solving. Chances are, the next time they run into a similar conflict, they will attempt the same approach, only a little less publicly.

As an alternative, the teacher might go over and take the book from the students, saying, *That's going to damage this book. Here, Carlos, you take it until lunchtime. William, you can have it for the rest of the afternoon.* The fact that the teacher does not personally attack the students will certainly make this response seem more attractive than the previous example, but there is still no opportunity for them to learn self-management from this conflict. Again, the book is safe and the fight has been broken up, but at what cost?

The *teacher* has absorbed the responsibility of solving the problem; however, in this example the solution is arbitrary and seems to punish one child while rewarding the other. The conflict has not been satisfactorily resolved in the students' minds even for the student who got the book (who probably has lost interest by this point). The teacher's intervention can actually escalate the negative feelings generated in the original argument. There has been no opportunity for negotiation and problem-solving; in fact, the teacher's behavior reinforces dependence and helplessness by suggesting that conflicts are solved by someone else.

As another option, the teacher might go over, take the book away and ask, *OK, what's going on here? Who started this?* Now, in our minds, it might seem logical that if we can just determine how this problem started and why it is happening, we can make the most impartial judgment. But beware of this temptation to jump into disagreements between kids. For one thing, the involvement can be incredibly tedious, time-consuming, and unproductive. For another, asking for background—especially with the intention of collecting data so that we can solve the problem, puts the responsibility on our shoulders. Most of the time, these questions model a need to fix blame and punishment—options that only serve to reinforce teacher power.

Beyond protecting the book and getting the noise to subside, the conflict is *not our problem*. Therefore, a more effective approach might sound like the following: *Stop! Books are not for pulling! Please put that on my desk until you can decide how it will be shared.* For an even greater chance of success, we might also remind them that resolving the problem means talking—not yelling or hitting.

This approach offers quite a few benefits. The teacher has dealt with the problem without attacking the students, dredging up judgments about personalities or past misdeeds, or lecturing or arguing. In addition, the teacher left responsibility for solving the problem with the ones who had created it. True, absolute silence has not been restored, but then, interpersonal problems don't get sorted out in silence.

This approach does not guarantee immediate quiet and harmony. In the above example, the teacher allowed the conflict to continue, but by setting limits and specifying a contingency, the students also had a chance to engage in a process that did not disturb anyone else. The only misbehavior addressed was the argument over the book, and the only consequence of the misbehavior was removing the object both students desired until a solution could be reached. There is no need for blaming or punishing, so the worth of the students, the value of their feelings, and the importance of their needs have been protected.

**The notion of consequence is consistent with win-win values; the idea of punishment is not.**

It is when a student misbehaves that our ability to withstand win-lose programming is challenged. It is easy to take negative behavior personally, especially if we are committed to building a positive learning environment. It takes a great deal of practice before we automatically respond to spilled paint by directing the child to a sponge instead of barraging her about her clumsiness.

The temptation to respond with power can be averted by looking for consequences—not punishments—to apply to student misconduct. Both may be effective for getting an immediate result, but each works in its own way.

To clarify, punishment is a form of consequence, but not all consequences are punitive. The notion of consequence is consistent with win-win values; the idea of punishment is not. Punishment may take the form of criticism, derision, humiliation, deprivation, isolation, physical pain, or the performance of some unrelated task. While factory-era teachers may have used punishment to curb undesirable behavior, they did so at the expense of the child's feelings, self-concept, and self-motivation, not to mention the long-term effects.

Punishment is often unrelated to the negative behavior and carries with it judgment and morality. Punishment makes little distinction between the student and his behavior, tending instead to rivet the worth of the child on one particular act. Punitive responses convey that not only is the behavior "bad," so is the student. Even simple mistakes or inconsequential forgetfulness can provoke a reaction that dramatizes the "wrongness" of the student.

> In a win-win classroom, consequences convey that a misbehaving student is still acceptable, valued, and welcome even if her behavior is not.

Consequences, on the other hand, focus exclusively on the behavior, not on previous behaviors or personality traits. Consequences remove the potential for conditional acceptance and approval that imply, *I like you (you're worthwhile) when* . . . In a win-win classroom, consequences convey the fact that a misbehaving student is still acceptable, valued, and welcome, even if his or her behavior is not.

Punishment may satisfy the teacher's need for control and power and is intended to deprive or hurt. It can therefore create resentment, hostility, and resistance, fueling negative teacher-student relationships, power struggles, and further disruptions. Teachers using punishment also model a way of dealing with conflicts by hurting or using force, especially when physical consequences are involved. This behavior implies that *you can get what you want as long as you are bigger, stronger, meaner, or more powerful.*

Punishment is also outcome-oriented, devoted primarily to short-term results, which allow students few opportunities to learn problem-solving skills on their own. Punishment endows the teacher with the primary responsibility for the solution of the problem and rarely goes beyond the immediate objective of getting the undesirable behavior to stop.

Consequences, however, do not attack or undermine the student's sense of worth and actually work to protect the child's needs for power and control within limits that do not hurt or deprive anyone else. Because non-punitive consequences are typically related to the behavior, and because they are not intended to hurt the student or bring pleasure to the teacher, students tend to be much more receptive to them. For this reason, consequences can eliminate power struggles because they emerge from the desire to protect everyone's needs and safety, not from the teacher's power.

When applying consequences, the teacher achieves the immediate objective, but also provides students access to processing steps not otherwise available. Thus, consequences connect the student's behavior to some intrinsic outcome—that is not the teacher's reaction—and reinforce the relationship between the student's behavioral choices and their outcomes. Punishment, on the other hand, teaches the student only to beware of the teacher's power. In addition, punishment relieves the student of responsibility—not only through the teacher's involvement with the *solution*, but also by suggesting that once the punishment has been served, the student is free to continue misbehaving until he or she is caught again. In this way, punishment actually reinforces teacher-dependence and interferes with opportunities for the student to develop self-control.

How can we respond constructively to student misconduct and still maintain our win-win intentions? Perhaps the most basic task, if not most difficult, is learning to separate the student from his or her behavior. While we may recognize on an intellectual level that a student is indeed more than simply a-person-who-forgets-library-books, it is easy for the misbehavior to overwhelm our attention, especially if it is something that has happened before. Likewise, we can intervene far more positively when we see a *poor choice* instead of a *possessed child*.

We must also decide if the behavior truly warrants our attention. Is the child creating actual problems for us or just getting on our nerves? Not all behaviors require consequences. One teacher complained about a fourth grader who sucked his thumb. She wanted to know what she could do to get him to stop. The behavior did not keep the student from doing his work and, since he always removed his thumb from his mouth before he started talking, it did not interfere with his ability to be understood. This behavior was not a problem for anyone except the teacher and it only bothered her because "it looks funny." In such cases, it may be better to focus on other, more important matters.

We can also avoid creating a major incident out of a small slip-up by minimizing our reactions. If a student knocks over a stack of papers and immediately bends down to pick them up, there is absolutely no reason for us to react. If the child creates a mess he doesn't know how (or is afraid) to clean up on his own, simple directions or an offer to help go much further than criticism, a lecture, or an impatient look. Some disruptions can be settled quickly and quietly, for example, by physical proximity (simply getting closer to the disturbance), non-threatening eye contact, or humor. If these behaviors achieve the cooperation we want, it's not necessary to involve ourselves further.

Efforts to set up no-fail situations at the outset are even more effective. Success orientation techniques such as providing limits in the beginning (*I will read each spelling word only once.*); giving special directions (*Here's how you can pour the juice without spilling it.*); or any other conditions we can set at the start will help students avoid accidents, omissions, or misunderstandings.

This is especially true about noise level. It's easy for students to lose sense of how loud they are getting, and it is impossible for us to give any specific limits (in terms of decibels). It is fair and helpful to let them know ahead of time, *I need for you to keep the noise down while I work on these papers. If I need to stop because of the noise, I will ask you all to return to your seats* (or whatever specific, related consequence will be likely to eliminate the problem).

But what about the problems even these measures fail to prevent? Once the student has violated the terms or limits of the contingency, the situation must change in order for the behavior to stop. Changing the situation requires an immediate and meaningful consequence. Unfortunately, there is often a great deal of time between the misconduct and a meaningful consequence; we tend, instead, to fill the gap with inconsequential responses, such as warnings and reminders. A warning may appear to have an immediate positive effect; however, the impact of warnings tends to be quite temporary and comes at a high cost. Even if the only drawback to this habit were the amount of time it wastes, it would still warrant some serious reconsideration.

**Warnings communicate a great deal of inconsistency on the part of the teacher.**

But warnings also communicate a great deal of inconsistency on the part of the teacher. We tend to be fairly arbitrary in our use of warnings as well as the number of warnings we are willing to give before we really let them have it. This response may come at any time (after maybe three or four reminders on a good day, after one or two if we are not in a very good mood) and is nearly always critical and punitive. When we get in the habit of giving reminders after or during a misbehavior, we are, in essence, devaluing the limits we place on the privileges we offer, inviting the students to not take them seriously.

Worse yet, we are also removing the power from the contingency itself and putting it back in our laps. When the warnings don't work, we blow up, reacting out of anger and frustration. When the consequence occurs immediately (the first time the misbehavior occurs), it is a function of the student's poor choosing; delayed by warnings, it becomes a function of the teacher's power.

Not all warnings are verbal. Frowning, finger-wagging, or writing a student's name on the board simply delay a meaningful consequence from occurring. As with verbal warnings, these reactions do little besides drawing attention to the misbehavior—and may have the opposite effect of what we intend—reinforcing what we are trying to stop. In addition, they rarely work because they don't qualify as meaningful consequences. In nearly all instances (except, perhaps, for the most diligent teacher-pleasers), continuing the negative behavior will be more need-fulfilling than avoiding Teacher's dirty looks.

Warnings seem convenient to us because it is actually easier to tell someone not to do something than it is to intervene. Warnings may seem generous and kind, and for a while protect children from experiencing the negative outcomes of their own behaviors. But this is exactly the long-range result we are trying to avoid. Each time warnings delay or replace consequences, they deny the student the opportunity to become more personally responsible for his or her behavior and less teacher-dependent. This means that we should not offer contingencies unless we are willing to insist that their terms be respected. (If we must give warnings, we need to do so before the negative behavior occurs; after that we must apply the consequence.)

**Each time warnings delay or replace consequences, the student loses an opportunity to become more responsible and less teacher-dependent.**

Other time-wasters include asking why a misbehavior has occurred, lecturing about the importance of cooperation, asking the student to repeat the rules, bringing up previous failures, engaging in discussions or arguments about the fairness of a consequence, or expressing our own feelings of disappointment or frustration.

A well-intended desire to stay positive (or lack of intervention techniques other than positive reinforcement) can be the source of yet another ineffective response. Positive reinforcement is effective only when a positive behavior has occurred. We certainly do not want to reinforce a misbehavior, and attempting to praise the student for something that is not occurring is dishonest, manipulative, and terribly confusing to students.

Applying consequences to a negative behavior is straightforward. Actions keep words to a minimum, so let the actions speak for themselves. Announce, *I will continue reading this story as soon as it gets quiet.* Then act—waiting, sitting quietly, with a neutral (not angry) facial expression. Fight the urge to repeat the announcement or embellish it with any further discussion. Either will sound as though you are trying to talk the kids into doing what you want. Silent refusal to read over the din of their conversation is far more powerful than anything else.

Yet even that may not get them quiet: students will choose the more need-fulfilling option and, in this instance, will only cooperate if their need to hear the story overrides their need to chatter. If the noncooperative behavior persists, it's time to close the book and get on with the day: *Please take your seats and get your math folders out. Let's try to finish this story tomorrow* (using the same neutral tone).

Now look at what we have accomplished. We have asserted our need for quiet attention when we read. We have connected their poor choice (talking) to a consequence (not getting to hear the rest of the story) that has nothing to do with our approval. We still accept the students, although we did not accept their behavior. We have not expressed anger, nor have we attacked the students or judged them. We've reinforced the limits that go along with the privilege without using power or force, and have also left the door open to try again at another time.

**We've reinforced the limits that go along with the privilege without using power or force and have left the door open to try again at another time.**

What about those situations in which only one or two students are disrupting the reading? It is obviously not necessary to stop reading altogether if the problem can be eliminated by asking individuals to leave the group (and perhaps return to their seats, another part of the room, or even another classroom, if prior arrangements have been established) until they can participate quietly. If these students can cease their disruptions by sitting and listening in a different location, there is no need to punish them by denying them the right to hear the story.

If there are, instead, only one or two students who are really trying to cooperate, we might want to provide some special option for them, since they will lose out if we can't continue because of the rest of the group. We can perhaps offer to loan them the book or put the rest of the story on tape for them to listen to at a later time.

And what about those situations in which we cannot really abandon what we are doing to move on to something else? Stopping in the middle of a special, high-interest activity is one thing, but we certainly would not want to drop every plan that does not sustain our students' attention. One first-grade teacher made a habit of stopping in mid-sentence as soon as she noticed that the kids had gotten distracted. Most of the time, her silence brought them back immediately. However, when the talking continued, she started looking at her watch. In the beginning, this behavior, by itself, had little meaning to the students, so she announced, *You know, we really need to finish this lesson. Your talking is taking up some of our work time. We've wasted one minute so far. After this, we'll have to take some time away from recess to get everything done.* From that point on, she would simply sit and wait, making hash marks on the board as each minute passed.

This strategy is not meant to suggest that we spend the entire year sitting and waiting for our kids to be quiet. But they might have to experience the consequences of their poor choosing before they can be expected to gain awareness of their misbehavior. This process is internal and often takes time. If the consequence is meaningful and significant, however, it usually does not take long, and it is the only way that can eventually stop the misbehavior from recurring.

For example, I taught one fifth-grade class just before lunch. The class seemed to take forever to clear their desks and get quiet before dismissal. I found myself giving them more and more time to get ready to leave until I realized that five minutes into the lesson I was starting to feel the pressure to clean up for a lunch period that was still 35 minutes away. Additional time obviously had not resolved the problem.

I decided to go back to the brief cleanup period I had always announced a minute or two before the lunch bell rang. And I also made sure they were aware of what would be happening ahead of time: *Listen, we've got a lot to cover today. Getting ready for lunch has been a problem for us, and today we'll have less time than normal. When we finish the lesson, I'll let you know that it's time to clean up. I'll say it once. After that, it's up to you. As soon as you clear your desks and get quiet, you can go down to eat.* I proceeded with the lesson as always and stopped at 11:58 to announce cleanup. From that point on I got busy with some papers on my desk.

Now I had thought that this clear, non-powering announcement, along with the threat of losing high-priority lunch and playground time, would clear up this silliness once and for all. Wrong. For some reason, it almost seemed to invite the kids to test how serious I was. (This may tell you something about my enforcement consistency prior to that day.) Students who hadn't been doing much of anything earlier in the period suddenly decided to get busy. Quiet kids started talking.

There was a part of me that wanted to get up and scream. It took every ounce of my self-restraint to stay calm and write a note down to the lunch service staff to mention that my class might be late . . . *however, please put their lunches out as usual.* I did not say a word. I didn't even glance at the clock. Every student had heard my announcement; every student had heard the lunch bell. After that, it was up to them.

Around 12:22, I noticed that it had gotten pretty quiet and when I looked up, the last student was clearing his desk and getting ready to go. Evidently some of them had noticed a few of their friends out on the playground and more than a few had started to get hungry. We arrived in the lunchroom two minutes later. The students were shocked to find their lunches had grown cold. Many students had not finished eating and only a few had gotten out the door to the play-ground when the bell rang to return to class.

Of course, the students were upset. I was not too thrilled myself about not getting a lunch break that day. But the sacrifice had been worth it. The next day, I had finished the lesson early to let them get started on their homework when I noticed, at 11:56, that each student was ready to be dismissed (I'm still amazed that they had all learned to tell time over-night). Now that they had initiated the cooperative behavior, I switched to reinforcement: *Looks like you're ready for dis-missal* (describing the behavior). Maybe we can get down there a little early today (what's in it for you). For the most part, that was the end of the lunchtime blues. Their coopera-tion became increasingly habitual and internalized; this was something one did to get to lunch on time, not to make the teacher happy.

**The lessons to be learned from one's misconduct come from the consequences of it, not from the power of the teacher.**

In factory-era authority relationships, misconduct is an invitation for the teacher to exercise power and control. Our immediate response, in this type of arrangement, is *What can I do to the student who has misbehaved? How can I teach him or her a lesson?* In a 21st-century classroom, the lessons to be learned from one's misconduct come from the con-sequences of the misconduct, not the power of the teacher. This also gives us the freedom to stop or remove the conse-quence once the student has stopped misbehaving and, if necessary, repair the damage his or her misbehavior has caused.

In the example above, the students missed lunch because of a poor choice they had made, not as a punishment for misbehaving. As soon as the students got themselves ready on time, there was no reason for the negative consequence (delaying lunch) to continue.

A punitive response would have us removing a privilege forever: *You'll never sit together again.* What does the stu-dent now have to lose? What will we do (or take away) if he does something really terrible? Consequences, on the other hand, allow the child to try again: *You each need to return to your seats. You can try working together again this afternoon.* or *Please leave the center now. You're welcome back here when you feel you can work without hitting.* Always leave the door open for the student to get it right.

When a misbehavior occurs because no previous limits had been set, it is certainly appropriate to back up and insert a new contingency: *Move those records, please. I forgot to tell you to be careful not to put them on the heater* or *And by the way, you have one minute to find a place to work and get busy.* From that point on, student violations require us to act. Once the announcement has been made, we are well within our rights to remove the records for the day or assign the indecisive student to a seat of our choice. These are the consequences of the students' inability to function within the previously announced limits. The records are removed so they don't melt; the student is assigned a seat so that the class can go on with its work.

Students are much more likely to respond cooperatively to *Please put that toy away until lunchtime* than *Put that thing away now!* (*Please* and *Thank You* are not just magic words for children.) On occasion, however, a student will resist even the most positively-stated request. There are a few tricks to avoiding a situation in which we back students into a corner. For example, switching from telling to asking can help. *You need to clear your desk. Where would you like to put that toy until lunchtime?* may be more effective than *Please put it away* because the former statement offers a greater number of positive choices. Telling or ordering may appear non-negotiable, but every do-it-or-else statement still offers a yes or no option. Offering two or more specific positive choices can also help prevent resistance and refusal: *Would you like to put that toy in my desk drawer or in your locker?* We still have the opportunity to step in with tighter limits or larger consequences if this approach is unsuccessful.

Adding a reason can also help: *Please put that toy away so that it can remain in this center (so that no one trips over it, or so that you can get back to work now).* Likewise, the word *until* offers hope and a promise of getting one's needs met at a later, specific time: *Please put that toy in your locker until your work is done (or until the dismissal bell rings).*

Finally, any time we recognize a student's desire to do something we're not willing to allow, we also promote cooperation: *This is a really nice toy. I know you wish you could play with it now. We need to get ready for the test and I think it might get in your way. Why not put it on my desk for now?*

> Every *Do-it-or-else!* statement still offers yes and no options, whereas two positive options can prevent resistance and refusal.

*You'll have some time to play with it when we're finished.* All of these techniques leave the student with a forward focus and an understanding that his or her needs are being considered and respected.

Our old win-lose patterns reappear most quickly when we confront an obstinate student. Unfortunately, if the child refuses to give up the toy despite all of our positive efforts, our first instinct is to immediately back up into power: *Give it to me now or I'll take it and you'll never see it again.* Giving in to the urge to overpower a student can undo a lot of the positive results gained by working towards a win-win environment.

A point-blank refusal can quickly turn into a no-win situation. The first casualty is often our perspective on the real issue, which, in this case, is that the student do the work— not that he obey the teacher. Backing off may mean sacrificing a short-term objective (getting him to give up the toy) to a long-term process (becoming responsible for doing his work regardless of temptations and distractions). But only in a win-lose classroom will your unwillingness to overpower or hurt a student make you come out a loser. Is it worth a power struggle that may or may not work (and then, if it does work, will do so for all the wrong reasons)?

Ideally, it's best to avoid power confrontations, but if one does come up, it's best to disengage quickly, if at all possible. We can always refuse to argue or try to force the student to cooperate: *I'm not about to try to force you to give up this toy. If you can work without being distracted by it, there's no problem. If not, I'll be happy to help you put it away. Keep in mind that your work must be finished in order for you to participate in this afternoon's activities* (go out for recess, go on to the next lesson, or whatever meaningful contingency is dependent on the work's completion). Then walk away.

If the student's behavior is only causing problems for himself or herself, the meaningful consequences of poor choosing will teach him or her far more than your power or anger. (And if the behavior is not causing a problem for anyone, including the student, there may not have been a need for your involvement in the first place.) Think, instead, of ways you can avoid similar incidents from occurring in the future. When cool heads once again prevail, announce: *You know, we've never needed a rule about toys before, so it's not fair for me to take them from you now. But keeping toys at your desk is interfering with your learning. I know these things are important to you. At the same time, your attention is important to me. You can still bring your toys to school tomorrow; however, they must stay in your locker or on my desk during class time. You can have them again during recess.*

No blaming, scolding, disappointment, or moralizing. We have gotten around the *I'll show you* mentality of a punitive, win-lose relationship because we don't need to cause someone to lose in order for us to win. We now have tighter limits and more specific contingencies. If the problem persists, further action may be necessary—a letter home requesting support for the rule or a total ban on toys. Please note, however, that as a win-win classroom develops, this type of resistance and rebellion will occur less frequently.

Once the students recognize your investment in their getting their needs met, these behaviors become increasingly pointless.

When we have done everything to make success possible and the student still makes a non-cooperative choice, a great deal of commitment and consistency is required to allow students to encounter the negative consequences of their poor choosing. If the child forgets his permission slip, he misses the outing. If she breaks or spills something in the classroom, she fixes, replaces, cleans up, or works off the damages, whether the damage was done accidentally or in anger. If he cannot control his urge to splash in the paint center, he does not get to play there for the rest of the day.

It may seem cruel to refuse to buy the student a meal the fourth time she forgets to bring in her lunch money (especially if you told her last time that she'd reached her credit limit), but for the sake of the child's growth toward responsible adulthood, there is no more loving response. Unless the child's life, health, or safety would be threatened by the consequence, being regularly allowed to experience the connection between her behavior and its outcomes encourages alternatives to blaming, helplessness, and irresponsibility, and assists the student in making more positive choices down the road. At no point is the child bad, stupid, or wrong; it's only the choice that could have been better.

The best consequences are those that start immediately and end when the misbehavior ceases. Because of pre-existing contingencies, Andrew can return to the group as soon as he feels he can control his urge to hit. Keisha can have another crack at the paint center tomorrow as long as she is willing to confine the paint to the paper. Donia can take a new library book home as soon as she brings back the pile she has at home. Even a student who has refused to do work—a behavior particularly hard for most teachers to deal

**Being regularly allowed to experience the connection between behavior and its outcomes assists the student in making more positive choices down the road.**

**Learning to react constructively in a negative situation is a process.**

with—is more likely to rethink the refusal if we can leave a way out: *You will need to decide if not doing the work is worth the consequences. In the meantime, I will leave your work on your desk in case you change your mind.*

Sounds great, but how can a busy and distracted teacher think so fast? Like all of the other skills discussed in this book, learning to react constructively in a negative situation is a process. These responses are difficult to plan, but as you move from blaming and punishing, and realign your interactions with win-win values, the rest follows.

When a student behaves destructively, hurting or endangering another student, property, or himself, our immediate goal is to intervene before further damage can occur. Very often, one word firmly spoken is enough. One upper-grade elementary teacher used to ask her students to *freeze* when she wanted their attention. They always enjoyed stopping in whatever position they were in—the sillier the better—until she would release them with *Unfreeze!* That technique was effective even in preventing various students from dropping crayons in the fish tank, following through on a punch or continuing to absent-mindedly carve gouges into the top of a desk. The word *Stop!* can also work, giving the student a chance to stop and think before any damage is done, rethink before he or she gets in any deeper, and back up and correct mistakes whenever possible. The break can also give us the chance to get the student's attention for further directions or consequences, if necessary.

When a student's behavior becomes extremely distracting or disturbing to others (without posing any actual danger to life or limb), our attention shifts to helping him or her settle down. It is hard to have a constructive dialogue or make a positive decision if one is near hysterics (this goes for both teacher and students). Frequently, a soft word of understanding or a gentle touch on the shoulder—which is possible only if we stay calm—can prevent an incident. We can also help the child by validating his feelings and offering an alternative to taking it out on the class—or on us: *I can see that you're upset. Why don't you get a drink and we can talk when you get back?* Asking the child to leave the environment can also help him or her disengage. This option is not a punishment for the angry student—it is a technique to help us stay calm, to protect the rest of the class, and to give the student a chance to catch his or her breath. Although it is unlikely to happen in a truly win-win classroom, if the student becomes too violent or dangerous to approach, send someone for help.

Very often, a student's outbursts are indications of a lack of effective alternatives to handling anger or frustration. Negative behaviors such as stealing, lying, or bullying can be signs that the student's control needs are not being met in more positive ways. Students who refuse to do assignments may be prompted by previous school failures, a genuine sense of *I can't* or a need for attention, albeit negative. Weak social skills can also account for a number of problems that arise.

Students who have consistently been on the losing end of win-lose authority relationships, who have already developed a habit of solving conflicts by hurting other people, need some concrete alternatives to lashing out. They also need time to develop trust in you and the system. A win-win classroom, with a measure of time and faith, can create the options, acceptance, and acknowledgment that will provide even the most severely damaged children opportunities to find more effective means of fulfilling their needs.

But a child who is out of control is not a good candidate for a lecture on self-management or a lesson on positive interaction with peers. We can make some time to build these skills, but not during a crisis. So, in addition to creating win-win options, modeling desirable behaviors, and persevering in patience and trust, we can also develop activities for non-conflict times to help students discover effective ways of meeting their needs without hurting anyone else. Techniques such as roundtable discussions, brainstorming sessions, and role-playing will help your students develop independence and problem-solving capabilities, as well as helping them learn to identify alternatives to antisocial behavior.

Such activities, supported by win-win teacher attitudes and behaviors, also help students to accept the range of feelings they experience without feeling guilty or wrong. Setting up real or imaginary conflict situations can offer opportunities to discuss *How do you feel when that happens? What do you wish you could do? What might happen if you did that? Aside from hurting this person, what do you want?* and *What are some other things you can do?* As with the problem-solving activities described in the previous chapter, these questions give kids practice at finding different ways of looking at the same situation, predicting outcomes, and identifying personal goals.

Even asking students to brainstorm on how they can get rid of their angry feelings (without pretending the anger is not there and without hurting anyone else) can provide a

**A win-win classroom can, with time and faith, provide even the most severely-damaged children opportunities to find effective means of fulfilling their needs.**

basis for self-management and assertive, self-caring communication. One teacher kept a pile of scrap paper handy near the trash can for students to crumple, rip to shreds, or write angry messages on (and then crumple or rip to shreds). Another kept a hall pass handy for any student who needed to take a break from the situation that was causing him or her frustration. Still another kept pillows to hit in a corner of the room. Another would take his kids out for a fun run when he felt tension build. These acceptable options sharply reduced the number of hurtful and disruptive incidents each teacher experienced.

Clearly, the more positive choices and contingencies available, the more the student has to lose when he or she does not cooperate. If you are working in a departmentalized system, you feel a greater degree of time pressure, as you are literally working from one bell to the next. Having students for only 45 minutes presents a number of problems not encountered in a self-contained classroom, not the least of which is having to go through the settling down and getting started phases with seven or eight groups of students. In these settings, it may be even more important to use choices and contingencies as motivators (and sources of consequences).

One middle-school teacher complained, I'm barely getting 20 minutes of instruction into a 40-minute class. How can I take the time to provide options and rewards? Yet her efforts at creating a win-win classroom, and particularly her attention to her students' needs and interests, paid off: she found that by building in time for need-fulfilling options, she actually increased instructional time by approximately ten minutes a day.

Although it requires a sharp change in focus from industrial values, increasing options for choices, negotiating, and offering rewards will surely improve motivation and cooperation, decrease negative behaviors, and give us built-in consequences when necessary. And, as we become more skilled at win-win teaching, we will find ourselves with better relationships with our students, more time for instruction, and far less stress in the workplace.

As teachers, we tend to emphasize misbehavior as the critical focus of our methods of discipline. The information in this chapter is important because it presents means for handling these behaviors. For this reason, several charts are included which highlight the points of the chapter, followed by activities which refer to this material. Take the time to read and work through these exercises. They may help you identify aspects of your teaching that need refocusing or reinforce what you already do in implementing 21st century discipline in your classroom!

# Punishment

- Win-lose.

- Power-oriented.

- Result of teacher's power, getting caught.

- Rarely related to the problem behavior.

- Equates student with behavior; attacks person.

- Related to worth of student; both behavior and student are wrong, unacceptable.

- Judgmental focus on morality of behavior.

- Arbitrary; often comes as a surprise; often no limits set beforehand.

- Teacher is responsible for correcting negative behavior.

- Teacher role: Policing, catching, blaming, disempowering.

- Lesson: Avoid power; invites students to get sneakier.

- Conflict Resolution Model: Force, hurt, deprive, threaten.

- Outcome-oriented.

- High cost to student's feelings, self-esteem, sense of control.

- High cost to teacher-student relationship.

- Student may respond with hostility, aggressiveness, rebelliousness. Can create additional conflict.

- Teacher may experience anger, disappointment, resentment, vengeance.

- Need-fulfilling to teacher.

- Often maintained after negative behavior stops.

# Consequence

- Win-win.

- Interaction-oriented.

- Result of student's poor choosing and behavior.

- Directly, specifically related to the negative behavior.

- Separates student from behavior; attacks behavior.

- Unrelated to student's worth—only behavior is wrong; student is still acceptable.

- Objective: focus on outcome or effect of behavior.

- Logical; limits and consequences set beforehand.

- Student is responsible for correcting negative behavior.

- Teacher role: Setting limits, intervention, facilitating student processing.

- Lesson: Personal responsibility; invites students to change behavior.

- Conflict Resolution Model: Negotiation, compromise.

- Process-oriented.

- Protects student's feelings, self-esteem, sense of control.

- Does not violate teacher-student relationship.

- Student more likely to respond with cooperation. Can avoid additional conflict.

- Teacher can remain neutral, calm, and accepting of student. Less stressful to all involved.

- Need-fulfilling to student and teacher.

- Can usually stop once student chooses more positive behavior.

# Guidelines for Handling Misbehavior

- Think prevention. Although no one can predict every possible opportunity for disaster, a large number of problems can be avoided by setting very specific limits ahead of time.

- When something comes up, try to isolate what's bothering you. Are you reacting to a personality trait or value conflict, or is the student's behavior actually interfering with the teaching or learning process?

- Attack the problem, not the person. Mentally separate the student from the behavior. It's the interruption that's annoying—not the student.

- Minimize your reaction. Count to ten, or at least to five. Use this time to remind yourself that you don't have to get angry, lecture, criticize, interrogate, or punish. (Often, you don't even have to get involved!) Staying calm can help you avoid compounding the problem at hand. A brief pause can also allow the student to resolve or correct the problem behavior on his own.

- Deal specifically with the behavior—not the morality of the behavior, previous incidents, or the personality behind the misconduct.

- If your reaction starts to create a win-lose (or no-win) situation, stop and back off: *Wait. This isn't the way I want to handle this.* If necessary—and possible—withdraw for a few seconds to regain your perspective.

- At all times, stay responsible for your actions and words. We are most vulnerable to negative adult behaviors in the presence of negative or disruptive student behaviors. Regardless of our commitment to maintaining a positive, win-win environment, there will be times we will most likely slip up and say or do something hurtful or destructive. Apologize and switch to more a constructive approach.

- Whenever possible, apply a meaningful consequence as soon as the misconduct occurs. Keep your tone and body language as neutral as possible.

- Whenever possible, invite the student to reclaim his or her privilege or possession as soon as the misbehavior ceases: *You may return to the group as soon as you can control your talking; You may continue playing with this game as soon as you finish cleaning up the area you just left.*

- If correcting the behavior will not give the student immediate access to the privilege or possession, let him or her know when it will be available again: *Please return to your seats. You can try working together again tomorrow. Please put the puzzle back on the shelf until you finish your seatwork.*

- Provide support, feedback, guidelines, and limits to help, but leave the responsibility for the student's behavior with the student.

- If instruction and activities would help in areas such as problem-solving, social interaction, or handling anger and frustration, save them for a non-crisis setting. Likewise, if you feel that you and your students could benefit from the administration or support staff (counselor, school psychologist, social worker), invite them to conduct or participate in these activities. These individuals may also be available to discuss particular problems and help you brainstorm possible win-win solutions, and will be especially helpful when you can provide documentation and don't attempt to dump the responsibility for the problem on them.

- In problem-solving activities and discussions, keep coming back to win-win: *How can we both get what we want?*

# Intervention Strategies

**Non-Productive**

Neutral/Non-Disruptive

**Intervention Strategy:** Contingency Contracting, Choices

**Goal:** Eliciting cooperative, constructive behavior process: Connecting low-probability behavior (what you want) to high-probability behavior (what the student wants): *If your work is done by noon, you can help out in the kindergarten. As soon as you clear your desks, we can watch the video. You may work together as long as you don't disturb anyone.*

**Caution:** To be effective, motivator (outcome) must be meaningful and need-fulfilling to the child.

**Counter-Productive**

Negative/Disruptive/Conflict

**Intervention Strategy:** Logical consequences with choices or contingencies.

**Goal:** Stopping the negative behavior, replacing with internally motivated cooperation.

**Process:** Drawing the student's attention to unacceptable behavior; requiring that the student change his/her behavior; accepting the student even though you do not accept the behavior. Stop behavior and present consequences, or, when possible, acceptable options. Relate consequence to misbehavior and leave the door open for the student to stop and replace negative behaviors. "You can have the book back as soon as you both agree on how you'll share it."

**Caution:** Once previously announced limits have been violated, apply consequences immediately. Avoid warnings and reminders after the fact. Do not ask why; ask instead what the student plans to do. Avoid punishing, giving advice or solutions, or taking responsibility for the student's problem.

Positive/Desirable                                              **Productive**

**Intervention Strategy:** Positive Reinforcement/
Recognition

**Goal:** Maintaining existing behavior, improving
likelihood of behavior recurring independently.

**Process:** Two-step process that connects the student's
positive choice to positive outcomes.

**Step 1:** Describe the positive behavior: *You put all the
science materials away.*

**Step 2:** Connect the behavior to what's in it for the
student: *Now you can go on to the next
activity.* Note: Outcome (step 2) must be need-
fulfilling for the student.

**Caution:** Avoid praise that connects the student's
self-worth to his or her choice or that reinforces
people-pleasing: *I really like you when . . . You're so
good when . . .* or *You make me happy when . . .*

# Teacher Behaviors to Avoid

- Punitive responses:
  — Yelling, blaming
  — Criticism, name-calling
  — Humiliation, derision
  — Deprivation of unrelated objects or privileges
  — Isolation, abandonment, conditional acceptance
  — Hitting, physical consequences
  — Sarcasm
  — Any task, look, word, or deed intended to hurt or get back at a student.

- Praising unrelated or previous behaviors to try to get the student to cooperate (or stop misbehaving).

- Ignoring misconduct that violates your safety, rights, or needs, or those of any of your students.

- Lecturing, moralizing, or attempting to "talk" the student into cooperating.

- Regularly calling on another teacher or administrator to handle your students' negative behaviors.

- Delaying a meaningful consequence with non-meaningful consequences (which may include warnings, threats, writing a student's name, or even a dirty look), when the contingencies have been set ahead of time.

- Reacting to or getting involved in situations which the students are resolving nondisruptively on their own.

- No-win power struggles; disempowering a student; backing a student into a corner.

Consider incidents or misbehaviors that have occurred
recently in your classroom. Then answer these questions.
Be sure to consult the charts on the preceding pages for
clarification.What were the misbehaviors?

**Activity**

In what way did these behaviors interrupt the teaching or
learning process?

What limits, if any, had been previously specified to
prevent such misbehaviors from occurring?

What else might you do to avoid similar future incidents?

What options does the student have for resolving or correcting these behaviors on his or her own?

What other options might you make available for similar future incidents?

In what ways have you been able to:

— isolate what was bothering you and avoid reacting to behaviors that were not actually disruptive?

— stay calm and minimize your reaction?

— mentally separate the student from the behavior; attacking the behavior without attacking the student?

In what ways have you been able to:

— deal specifically with the behavior, regardless of the morality of the behavior, previous incidents, or the personality behind the misconduct?

— back off and shift to a more positive approach if you felt yourself moving toward no-win or win-lose?

— stay responsible for your actions and words?

— apply a meaningful consequence as soon as the misconduct occurred?

In what ways have you been able to:

— maintain a neutral tone of voice and a nonaggressive body posture?

— leave the door open for the student to return to the positive contingency (participation, using particular equipment, access to a privilege)?

— leave the responsibility for the student's behavior with the student?

— keep coming back to win-win?

What have you done to avoid the following negative
teacher behaviors?

— Any punitive response (task, look, word, or deed)
  intended to hurt or get back at the student.

— Praising unrelated or previous behaviors to try to get
  the student to cooperate (or stop misbehaving).

— Ignoring misconduct that violates your safety, rights,
  or needs, or those of any of your students.

— Lecturing, moralizing, or attempting to "talk" the
  student into cooperating.

— Regularly calling on another teacher or administrator
  to handle your students' negative behaviors.

— Delaying a meaningful consequence with
  meaningless consequences.

What have you done to avoid:

— Reacting to or getting involved in situations which the students are resolving nondisruptively on their own.

— No-win power-struggles; disempowering a student; backing a student into a corner.

Which of the above negative responses have been most difficult for you to avoid?

How have your efforts at developing a win-win classroom environment, focusing on meeting student needs, and providing a variety of positive options and contingencies affected the incidence of negative and disruptive student behaviors?

How have these efforts contributed to your own growth, wellness, and enjoyment of your work?

In what ways have your students shown growth in:

— meeting their needs for attention, recognition, and belonging?

— finding nondisruptive means of dealing with anger and frustration?

— finding nondisruptive means of getting their control needs met?

— interacting positively with other students?

— respecting and accommodating your needs?

What are your plans to further enhance your growth— and your students growth—in these areas?

Section Four

# Working the System

# 17 Building and maintaining a support network

Naturally, up to this point we have focused on relationships between teachers and their students. Yet teaching can sometimes leave us feeling isolated from everyone *except* our students. It is important to remember that each of us is also a part of an adult school community that includes other teachers, administrators, support staff, and parents. Even if our contact is infrequent, the quality of these relationships has an impact on our attitudes, performance, mental health, and sense of belonging. With support from the adult community, even the most difficult students seem less challenging. On the other hand, lack of support can make us feel completely alone. And negative relationships with other adults can make life miserable within the ideal classroom.

Thus, building a support network involves consciously connecting with other adults not just for solving problems, but for feedback, encouragement, and renewed perspectives throughout the year. It means applying win-win objectives and behaviors to prevent and resolve conflicts with other adults. And it means reciprocating to others, as well.

The task also requires some groundwork. Seeking answers to questions such as the following helps: Who's out there? What does each resource have to offer? At what point does a resource want or expect to be included? What sort of approach works best with each? How much background work do I have to do to make it more likely that the person will be willing to help? What can I do to make his or her help more meaningful and effective? Which of his/her needs can I accommodate to minimize conflict at work?

Parents and guardians, for example, can provide a great deal of support and reinforcement. For the most part, they want to know what is happening in school, how their children are doing, and how the parents can help. They tend to be far more enthusiastic and positive in their support when informed, included, and welcomed in classrooms, and when their interest in their children's well-being is respected. Unfortunately parent-teacher relationships rarely attain their maximum potential. Often both parties complain of a lack of contact *unless there is a problem.* If this has indeed been the case with the parents and guardians of your students, imagine how effective a more positive approach can be!

Be sure to get acquainted early in the year, either by note, phone, in-school conferences, welcome meetings, or home visits. Keep first meetings positive. Make a point of keeping in contact on a regular basis. An occasional newsletter keeps parents informed about new projects, activities, and objectives, and provides a showcase for students' contributions. Parents are especially likely to read newsletters that have been prepared by their children.

Checklist progress reports can tell a parent or guardian about the specific strengths and positive behaviors their child exhibited that week. These weekly reports, which need not take more than five or ten minutes to complete for an entire class, communicate your interest in and commitment to their child's success [1]. (It may seem that your usual correspondences never get home, but somehow these *good notes* do manage to get there.)

If you teach several classes, weekly progress reports may not be practical. Select one or two classes which would benefit most from parent support and send reports home. You can wait for something special to happen to send a note home, but make sure you send one for each child in the class. For the most part, try to communicate with parents at least once every two or three weeks. (Checking off students' names on a roll sheet as you send notes home helps you avoid missing less visible students.) These messages are appreciated, not only by parents, but also by students and administration as well. The notes tend to build good home-school relationships and invite regular, positive, parent involvement. If problems arise, it's then possible to approach the parent within the framework of frequent and positive prior contacts.

If you call to let parents know about a problem, state that as the purpose of the call and inform them of your goals and plans. You might ask if they have any ideas or suggestions. Above all, avoid blaming, unloading, or asking them to solve the problem for you. Don't use the call either as a punishment for the child's misbehavior, or to ask the parent to apply consequences for a behavior that the parent did not witness.

**In all instances keep relationships and interactions professional.**

If a student is experiencing difficulty with school work or social behavior, or is demonstrating behaviors that are interfering with potential success in school, get in touch with the parents right away. Don't allow yourself to be placed in the embarrassing position of having to explain why you did not contact the parents until the behavior had become a problem.

In all instances, keep relationships and interactions professional. Focus your discussions on the child. Avoid mentioning other students, parents, or professionals.

School administrators are also valuable resources and can make the difference between a great year and one fraught with obstacles. One of the most common complaints from administrators is that teachers rely on them to take care of routine discipline problems and annoyances. Few principals enjoy being called on to punish students, especially for something like chewing gum, talking out, being unprepared, or acting out as the result of the teacher's negative or hurtful behavior.

Even if your principal enjoys playing disciplinarian, you will not be well-served by relying on him or her to take care of misbehaviors. For one thing, it is nearly impossible for someone outside the direct interaction to apply fair and meaningful, win-win consequences that directly relate to the incident. Sending a child to the principal's office, therefore, tends to be a punitive win-lose option that rarely has anything to do with the misbehavior. Instead, it is intended to hurt or retaliate, and, at the very least, conveys a lack of acceptance of the student.

Referring misbehaving students to the principal communicates—to the administration, staff, and the students—that you are unable to resolve your own conflicts, and also models dependence on someone else to fix personal problems. If we want to get the student out of the room in order to defuse or break up a conflict, the office may be a fine place for the student to go to calm down, but beyond requesting the use of the space for that specific purpose, the principal need not be involved in the intervention nor resolution. (If the principal cannot resist getting involved, you and the student will probably fare better by asking the student to go to another classroom, the library, the hall, or some place nearby.)

Again, assume responsibility for what goes on in your classroom. Invite your principal to observe, make recommendations, point you to the best resources, clarify available options, or help you brainstorm solutions. If you think that the principal could be helpful in some way, approach him or her with a plan. Be specific about the problem, your objective, and what the administrator can do to help. Attempt to resolve problems on your own. The administrator is then far more likely to be supportive when really needed.

**The support staff is far more receptive when asked to help with—not solve—the problem for you.**

Finally, make sure the office gets a copy of anything you send home (such as announcements, newsletters, or general correspondence). Administrators also appreciate documentation: any time you keep track of parent contacts, incidents with students, or student achievement, diagnoses, placement, and progress, you also protect the administrator. If you are sending individual progress reports, as suggested above, let the principal know about it. It's also a good idea to inform him or her of special plans or events. The fewer surprises that end up in the office, the more supportive the administrator will be.

The support staff, particularly the school psychologist, counselor, health care resource, and social worker, can provide a tremendous amount of assistance during the year. They, too, are far more receptive and helpful when approached to help—not solve the problem for you. If you approach a support staff member to help with a particular student, be specific about the problem, as well as how you want that person to help.

In general, the support of these staff members is sought in regards to individual students. The more information you can provide, the more help you are likely to receive. Keeping track of student performance and behavior with a variety of data-collection techniques can provide you with valuable documentation. A student file which contains work samples, anecdotal records (brief notes describing a students' language, performance, interests, behaviors, strengths, or interactions, usually with regard to some specific incident or observation), and interest inventories present a more detailed and objective picture of a student than simple grade sheets and general comments [2].

Such information can also be essential in generating administrative support for special testing, help, or placement. Data collected from a variety of sources about a student helps the administration or support staff make decisions about what they can do or recommend to help. A diverse student file adds to your professional image and is far more likely to get positive results than simply telling the school psychologist that *Adrian is driving me nuts.*

Other teachers can be valuable resources in a number of ways. In addition to providing ideas for activities, materials, and instructional techniques, they also serve as models for teaching and discipline strategies. Other teachers may be willing to observe you and provide feedback for specific skills you are trying to develop. They can give you helpful background on specific students, as well as some perspective on problems you encounter. They can also be great allies for projects that involve a grade level, department, or the entire school, or anything that requires administrative or community support.

You probably have far more contact with teachers than any of the other resources mentioned previously, and have a great deal to gain by building strong relationships with this segment of your support network. If you are new to a staff, you may not be familiar with existing relationships, power structures, and traditions. It may take a while to determine who is willing to share materials, who is interested in your ideas, and who is most likely to offer encouragement and support when you are having a bad day. There will also be times that require cooperation from other teachers simply so that you can do your job effectively, such as the need to schedule the use of certain equipment or to cooperate on a project too large to handle alone.

Other staff members, such as the cafeteria staff, school secretary, and custodian will appreciate your efforts at building and maintaining positive relationships. These individuals are essential members of the school staff who can make a great difference in the quality of your life at school.

Finally, the community is full of resources—people and places—that can enrich your instruction, provide background information, or lead you to a wealth of materials. The professional community, including teacher resource centers, professional libraries, colleges and universities, and various educational organizations can likewise contribute to your personal and professional growth.

As in any relationship, the basics apply. We always fare better when we act the way we want to be treated, take time out to show appreciation, ask directly, and are willing to give in return. The same win-win characteristics that apply in working with kids in the classroom apply to professional adult relationships.

Yet getting students to cooperate is slightly different from generating cooperation from other adults. In a win-win teacher-student relationship, the teacher is ultimately accountable for the classroom's emotional climate, the criteria for acceptable behavior, and for the methods chosen to encourage positive student behavior. Peer relationships, even those in which one adult has more power, are not nearly as clear-cut.

Too often, teacher stress and burnout involves problems with other adults. Problems arise from time to time whenever people work together. But learning when and how to react can save you from personal feelings of anger, frustration, powerlessness, or self-righteousness, and can also help you avoid ending up on the receiving end of suspicion, alienation, or hostility.

When something comes up, be direct. Many people dance around a problem and never get close enough to actually resolve it. Consider Mr. Gordon, who is angry at Mrs. Hartz. He tells Mr. Sanchez, Ms. Rodgers, and Mrs. Chasler; he mentions it to the principal, the custodian, his wife, and the cat. He tells everyone except Mrs. Hartz. Complaining does not solve his problem and may even compound whatever is wrong, especially if it gets back to Mrs. Hartz.

People perpetuate conflict by complaining rather than confronting, and they do so for a number of reasons. Sometimes they secretly hope that someone else will solve the problem for them. (Is this why Mr. Gordon mentioned it to the principal?) Some people avoid coumunicating because they believe in some clairvoyant connection (*Well, she should have known!*) or because of a perceived risk (*She won't like me*). More often, people shy away from a direct approach because they don't believe they have the power to change things.

Successful relationships do not mean that you never have any problems with people. But they do require a belief in the power to influence your life and make choices for your behavior. This fact becomes especially clear in the language and tone you select when you confront someone directly.

When you encounter a problem in which someone else's behavior is keeping you from doing or enjoying your job, the first response is often reactive. It is hard to be objective when the noise from next door hinders your teaching or when someone is using equipment you reserved. When you find that Mrs. Patton is using the projector, and the only other time it will be free before you must return the film is when your students will be in another class, your initial reaction may be somewhat emotional: *Can't she read the schedule?*

Beyond the initial feelings, as with your interactions with students, you have several options. If you slip back into powering, you might confront Mrs. Patton and demand that she shut off the projector immediately. (After all, you have the schedule on your side.) But regardless of how justified you are, you have just backed the other teacher into a win-lose situation, and it can cost you plenty. This powering approach considers only your needs; it is likely to create hostility, resentment, and strong resistance with someone who might have tried to work out the problem. If you get the projector, is it worth the emotional strain and future alienation?

**In a win-win approach, you take responsibility for meeting your needs while considering the needs of others.**

The possibility of making a scene—or an enemy—can lead to the opposite win-lose scenario. In this instance, you decide to not mention it, either because it probably would not do any good or it would just create greater problems. In the meantime, your need for the projector falls by the wayside. That may be OK if the film is really less important than your need to avoid a confrontation with Mrs. Patton, but what about a more serious situation? What about the noisy class next door that's disturbing you and your students? The why-bother approach is adequate as long as you can live with its consequences. Although, assuming the victim stance often masks the same *how dare she* feelings that prompted a power approach, it probably appears as ineffective complaints, helplessness, or manipulation to see if Mrs. Patton will relent out of pity.

You can try a win-win approach. In this case, you actively take responsibility for meeting your own needs while considering the needs of another person. By saying to Mrs. Patton, *I think we have a problem; I signed up to use the projector this period.*, you are simply stating the situation. You have stated the problem without attacking Mrs. Patton. You have also side-stepped the emotional issues. *I don't see any other time the projector will be free before the film goes back. Is there some way we can work this out?* This statement gives the other teacher additional information, allows her to comment, and puts you both in a position to cooperate.

In the same way, the noise-level problem must be approached with statements that neither destroy that teacher's credibility as an instructor nor invalidate her worth as a person. Describe the problem in terms of your own needs: *I'm about to give a test to my class and need a bit more quiet, please. We're having a hard time hearing the movie.* By using the word *I*, you have taken responsibility for your needs and for what is disturbing you. Avoiding the word *you* also focuses on the problem—not the person.

As in teacher-student relationships, the best way to resolve a problem with other adults is to prevent it from occurring in the first place. It helps if you are good at anticipating, but even more important is the realization that people rarely understand implicitly what you want, need, or think. All of us are creatures of our experiences and everyone's experiences are unique. This means that what may be obvious, logical, and right to you, may never enter another person's head.

Suppose, for example, that you and Ms. Bender plan to combine classes for a special project. You have observed that she seems to favor certain children. To prevent this from happening in your work together, you tell her that it is important to you that everyone has a chance to share opportunities, materials, and responsibilities. This statement probably will not cause Ms. Bender to restructure her value system, but she may think twice before she assigns particular jobs to favored children—at least while you are around. Even if your request doesn't affect her behavior, you have the privilege of knowing that you have done your best with what you can control—*your* behavior.

Anticipation and courtesy can help avoid problems. Ask ahead of time if neighboring teachers will be bothered by a noisy activity in your room after lunch. Find out when the library will be free for your students next week. Establishing a strong support network and consistently modeling win-win in your adult relationships might help your colleagues become more considerate of your needs and how they might be affected by the plans and choices they make.

One final thought. If you have your interpersonal and conflict-resolution skills in order, you may nonetheless run into problems if the adminstration is not supportive of your intentions. The absence of adminstrative support can sometimes degenerate into a no-win situation. You have a much better chance of minimizing resistance if you: build your win-win environment within the confines of school policies, keep the prinicpal informed of what you are up to, maintain a high degree of professionalism, keep in touch with parents, take responsibility for solving problems with students, and get results—especially if those results are documented. A difference in philosophy and approaches to motivation can avoid drawing fire from above, if you are not causing problems for the administration.

---

[1] For more details about building positive home-school relationships with newsletters and progress reports, see *Being a Successful Teacher,* Bluestein. David S. Lake Publishers, Belmont, CA, 1988.

[2] Ibid (for information about data collection tools and strategies).

**Activity**   The Support Network

What have you done to build support relationships with the following groups of people?

Administration:

Support staff:

Other teachers:

Parents:

Other school staff:

Other community resources:

How have the support relationships contributed to your mental health?

Administration:

Support staff:

Other teachers:

Parents:

Other school staff:

Other community resources:

In what ways have you involved the following people in your discipline program?

   Administration:

   Support staff:

   Other teachers:

   Parents:

   Other school staff:

   Other community resources:


What have you done to maximize the ability of these individuals to help?


In what ways have these people contributed to a win-win classroom environment?

   Administration:

   Support staff:

   Other teachers:

   Parents:

   Other school staff:

   Other community resources:

Conflict Resolution

Think about a situation in which your needs were in conflict with the needs of another adult in school or out. Regardless of how you actually approached or resolved the conflict, use the following questions to explore the situation, its various dimensions, and possibilities involved: [3]

Your needs (what you wanted):

His/her needs (what he/she wanted):

The conflict (why his/her needs interfered with yours):

Your initial feelings or reactions:

Describe the powering (you win, he/she loses) options you considered (or might have considered):

Describe the probable short-term outcomes of implementing these solutions:

Describe the probable long-term outcomes of implementing these solutions:

What would have been the probable outcomes of simply ignoring the problem?

Short-term:

Long-term:

List any other people you talked to regarding this problem before you actually confronted the other person involved:

What was the purpose of these discussions?

In what ways did these discussions help you resolve the problem?

In what ways did (or could) these discussions create new problems?

How long did this problem exist before you actually confronted the person directly?

If your approach was not immediate, what held you back?

Brainstorm a variety of possible win-win solutions in which you and the other person can eventually manage to get what you each want. (If that is not practical or possible—say, you're both fighting over the last M & M—how can you resolve the conflict in the best interests of all concerned?)

What are the probable short-term outcomes of the win-win solutions you suggest?

What are the probable long-term outcomes?

In what way did your actual approach consider the needs and feelings of the other person?

Describe the other person's response. In what ways (or to what degree) were you successful at preventing the situation from becoming no-win?

In what ways are you satisfied with the way you handled your feelings about this problem?

In what ways would you have like to have behaved differently?

In what ways are you satisfied with the way the situation was resolved?

If the problem was not resolved to your satisfaction, how could it be resolved in a better way?

Describe any new problems created by the solution.

How can the new problems or your dissatisfaction with the solution now be resolved in the best interests of all involved?

How do you plan to handle similar future conflicts?

[3] You may want to use some of these questions in your discussions and activities on conflict resolution and relationship building with your students.

# 18    Taking care of yourself

**I**f teaching involved only planning and presenting content, it would still be an extremely demanding job. But consider the paperwork that requires secretarial skills, the movement and organization that call for management expertise, the emotional needs that oblige a teacher to serve as a counselor, or the boo-boos that demand the role of nurse. Every facet of teaching, as fulfilling and enriching as it may be, also depletes.

As if these demands were not enough, the habit of setting unrealistic expectations for ourselves can be terribly stress-producing in itself. Becoming a great teacher is a developmental process that does not always jibe with the image of how we want to be. Even if we have been teaching for years, as long as we are committed to excellence, we will always be looking for new tricks to try and new ways to grow.

One of the greatest things about teaching, which may also be the most challenging, is the fact that there is always something new for us to deal with: different groups each year; a student who changes the chemistry of the current group; content and programs; updated hardware and equipment; different grades or subjects to teach; or strategies, ideas, and innovations that we encounter for the first time. And every time we try something that is new to us or face a different group of kids, we run the risk of presenting lessons that do not go quite the way we plan. This is part of the process!

A positive focus is not limited to our observations of our students. For example, during my first year of teaching, one of my professors from the university came out to observe. We had worked together in the past and it was very important to me that he be impressed with my work (after all, wouldn't his approval make me a good teacher and a generally worthwhile human being?) Of course, he came in on a day that everything possible was going wrong. The ditto machine broke and one of my handouts wasn't ready. The students did not understand my instructions and did the activity incorrectly. I attempted to show a filmstrip and the bulb burned out. When I finally got the kids' attention at the end of the period, one of the blinds let go and dropped with a crash.

*You know, your flag looks great!*

By the time the kids left, I was in shambles. I sat and sobbed, offered my resignation, and made secret plans to apply to dental school or marry someone very rich instead. I even started cleaning out my desk and suggested that he try to find a replacement who could actually teach. I had a very bad case of the *I can'ts* and he listened and nodded patiently.

Finally, he got up and said, *You know, your flag looks great!*

I stopped, stunned. My flag? I couldn't even reach the flag without a ladder.

*That's a good start. We'll work on the rest. Don't worry, you'll be fine. I'll see you next week.* After which he left.

Now here was a person able to look beyond the mistakes—some of which I could have controlled better, others that were completely out of my control and impossible to predict—to the one thing I had not messed up. My flag looked great! Once I recovered, I started noticing that my flag did look pretty good; that the materials I had prepared were done well; and that the filmstrip I had selected had been interesting, applicable, and well-sequenced. I might not have seen my other successes if he had mentioned them, but the comment about the flag certainly got my attention!

I can. Maybe.

Not terribly illustrious beginnings, I admit. But the lesson was not lost on me, even if it did take a while to surface.

This example illustrates another danger of coming from an industrial-era background that reinforced achievement over effort, product over process, and perfection over everything else. No wonder looking good and expressing authority (product) seemed more important than seeing the opportunities in each experience to become a better teacher (process)! It is also easy to see how we can be either extremely arrogant or extremely hard on ourselves. Both are based in denial—one of our vulnerability, the other of our capability; and both deny our needs to continually grow and develop as professionals.

In sorting through this experience, I also realized that if I want to focus on my students' strengths and abilities, I have to learn to do so for myself. This is one aspect of self-care. Another is learning to detach oneself, when necessary, from self-destructive or difficult students, and from the demands of the job.

Because the planning and preparation of lessons, activities, materials, and environments can consume so much time—especially during the first few years of a teacher's career, in a new setting, or at a new grade level—it is not uncommon for hobbies, recreational reading, or other outside interests to shift to a lower place on a teacher's list of priorities. Teaching requires a great deal of giving on many levels. True, there can be a great deal of satisfaction in putting out so much time, creativity, physical and emotional energy. However, many teachers often reach the end of the day with little to give back to themselves.

Teaching tends to attract helpers and nurturers. Although it is not always the case, most teachers identify heavily with the progress and performance of their students. We don't want to see people we care about fail—especially if we believe that their failure reflects on us. While these feelings may seem natural and caring, they may also create very negative consequences, for both us and the students. For example, when our professional identity and feelings of success are tied up in the choices students make, our focus can shift from success orientation for the sake of the students to rescuing them from failure for the sake of ourselves. If our sense of our teaching self is too closely connected to our students' behavior and achievement, we may become resentful and punitive when sincerity and commitment do not work.

A very important skill in self-caring is learning to separate things we can change, control, or influence from those we can't. Unfortunately, some of the most frustrating experiences in our lives come from events we can't do much about. We get moved to a grade we didn't want to teach. Our normal ride to work takes twice as long because of a construction project. The parents of our students don't read to them (or, perhaps, are guilty of serious neglect).

True, we can transfer to a new school, go back and get a degree in architecture, leave the house two hours early to avoid rush hour, or buy a home closer to where we work. We can make home visits and start a home literacy education project in our spare time. There are always options in any situation, but the more removed something is from our direct control, the greater the discrepancy between the energy we need to effect change and the amount of change our energy actually promotes. Instead of succumbing to frustration, burnout and few results, we can choose instead to channel our efforts in a high-impact direction and make constructive choices about the things we *can* control.

If we have learned anything about win-win interactions we know that students—along with everyone else—fall in that great gray area between those things that are completely out of our control (like the weather) and those that we control completely (like how often we floss). Throughout this book we have seen how the behaviors, attitudes, and language we choose in interacting with students can make it more likely that they will behave in a certain way, but at no time do we actually control them.

So when we run into disappointments—lessons that fall flat, students who drop the ball, administrators who simply can't see the beauty in what we were trying to do—it is tempting to lump all the incidents into one pile-of-things that discredit us as instructors. But it's not necessary. We can, as we have seen, take care of everything under our control and still have things go wrong.

Somewhere between beating ourselves for our failures and becoming completely indifferent is a very loving place called Letting-go. This is that nice middle ground where we realize that the final choice rests with the other person. We sometimes come to this place when we have tried everything and realize, nevertheless, that our attempts to control the other person have endowed us with more responsibility, self-righteousness, anger, and stress than we can comfortably bear.

Every now and then we run into people who appear committed to their own destruction or invalidation, people whose self-concepts are so low and so fragile that they feel safest when they constantly create opportunities to fail (doing so proves that they are right about themselves). Of course we try to help, to boost poor self-concepts, and encourage success. In many instances, patience and persistence can win out.

However, when our efforts fail, and when the failures of our efforts take more from the individual, ourselves, and the rest of the class than they actually contribute, it is time to turn the problem back to the student or other person. It is possible that nothing may work. The point is that we keep on trying and we give ourselves credit for trying; but the difference is that we have disengaged ourselves from the results. In this case, not only is the student worthwhile and valuable despite his or her behavior, so are we.

Our professional self-concept can be rather fragile at times. If the bulk of our experiences has been with factory-era authority relationships, we have years of practice judging ourselves against other people's standards and reactions. If approval from others is a high priority, we become extremely vulnerable to the power-oriented teacher who does not sanction our methods, to the parent who wants his child in a different fourth grade, or to the fact that the other social studies teacher is twenty pages ahead. Learning to operate from internal needs and standards promises a great deal of freedom; however, doing so requires some relearning, refocusing, and letting go of old beliefs that no longer work for us [1].

Regardless of the quality of the support networks you build, the bottom line in responsibility for self-care is self. Fortunately, even with none from outside, you can draw upon support from within. Taking care of yourself means identifying which challenges deserve your time and attention and determining whether or not you need to get involved.

For example, it's easy to allow classroom attitudes, where most things *are* your business, to become school attitudes, where many things are not. Wherever you teach, you will find people who work differently than you. And while you may find the differences annoying, your involvement is not required unless the other adult keeps your approach from working [2].

In addition, seeing two colleagues in conflict with each other, knowing another teacher who is having problems with the principal, or working with someone who can't quite get it together can engage you almost by accident. Whether hooked by conflicting values or just trying to help, whenever

**Learning to operate from internal needs and standards requires relearning, refocusing, and letting go of old beliefs that no longer work for us.**

we jump into a situation that does not truly concern us, we risk taking on additional stresses and problems.

The cost of unsolicited intervention, particularly in the form of judgments or criticisms, can be high. Even if you are asked to help, your assistance may not be welcome if it is not the kind of response the person wants to hear.

**Remember the best help is often letting people solve their problems.**

You can be supportive of another teacher and still recognize where his or her responsibility begins and ends. Listening, accepting, acknowledging, modeling, providing information and materials, and helping that person think through possible solutions may help—without placing responsibility for the problem on your shoulders. These strategies neither attack the other person nor attempt to impose your value system on them. Curbing the inclination to rescue, save, or fix another person frees you to be there for someone without becoming enmeshed in his or her conflicts. Remember, the best help is often letting people solve their own problems.

Learning to detach is especially important if you become involved in a no-win situation. If you have been unable to resolve a conflict to your satisfaction, the next step is to suggest arbitration. If Mrs. Patton is unwilling to work with you to settle the problem with the projector, you might say, *I understand that the schedule was developed to avoid problems like these. Would you prefer to work this out with the building committee?* Notice that this statement is not intended as a threat—you have simply presented another option.

Unfortunately, when you turn a problem over to someone else, you almost always turn over the responsibility for a solution to that person as well. The advantage is that the third party can usually see things more clearly and objectively and may suggest options that didn't occur to either of the people involved. The disadvantage is that a mediator may well solve the problem as quickly and conveniently as possible (or in terms of what is most need-fulfilling to him or her), with less regard for the specific needs of both parties. Finally, an outside person may have difficulty remaining objective, avoiding power decisions, or sticking with relevant issues. There is always the chance that the third party will make things worse, so select your arbitrator cautiously.

Sometimes persistence can overcome a seemingly no-win situation. With the support of your principal, custodian, and the students' parents, it still may be hard to convince a repairman that you and your students really need to have the heater fixed, but when that person recognizes that he or she will no longer be bothered by three calls a day once it works, you are more likely to get results. Be pleasant if you choose to be persistent and, if possible, always make a point of telling the other people involved what is in it for them to cooperate.

Unfortunately, you may not be able to directly solve every problem with another individual. A no-win situation like this may arise from a loss of perspective or a personality conflict. For example, Mr. Collins was scheduled to be observed by Mrs. Willard, the principal, who came by the class when the teacher was presenting an activity designed to reinforce a particular reading concept. Mrs. Willard was concerned that Mr. Collins' activity was not in the teacher's guide and asked that he use the guide exclusively.

Under protest, Mr. Collins did use the guide, almost word for word, in his planning. He then came under attack for being unoriginal. Mr. Collins was clearly caught up in a no-win power struggle. He told Mrs. Willard that he was getting conflicting messages from her. *I'm trying to follow your suggestions, but it seems that I can't do anything without being criticized. Is there something I'm not understanding?* Mrs. Willard responded that he was being too sensitive. When pressed to elaborate her expectations, she refused further discussion.

What options does Mr. Collins have? He may try several different approaches, depending upon his need for approval, his tenure and mobility within the system, his self-assurance and documentation, his career goals, his ability to enjoy positive outcomes of teaching despite Mrs. Willard, and his sense of humor. He may choose to enlist parents, colleagues, and his union to fight. He might continue trying to persuade the principal to give more specific information or at least attempt to understand his approach. He might agree with Mrs. Willard to her face and devote his energy to beating, or side-stepping, the system for as long as he can get away with it. He may go with the flow to try to keep Mrs. Willard off his back.

But considering the deliberate lack of support and intent to undermine the teacher's confidence, Mr. Collins probably will not have a long-term relationship with Mrs. Willard. In such a painful no-win situation, seeking a position elsewhere may be the most emotionally cost-effective option.

When our jobs—for whatever reasons—become a stressful bundle of obstacles and conflicts, we may need to re-evaluate whether the payoffs and benefits are more need-fulfilling than the negative aspects of the work. The times we are most vulnerable to burnout, fatigue, depression, and poor self-concept at times when no other options seem available (low sense of personal empowerment).

One of the most powerful behaviors we can engage in for self-protection is the conscious act of exploring options: a different grade level, another school or district, arbitration, a year off to finish a degree, or the pursuit of an entirely different career. Sometimes it can help relieve some of the pressures in even the most negative situations to realize that we are not trapped and acknowledge we just have not yet found a more need-fulfilling option for ourselves.

We also need interests in our lives, besides teaching, to give us balance and perspective. Being good at what we do comes easier when we are in shape physically and mentally. Activities that are also stress-reducing can serve us best. Taking a class in our field, pursuing a hobby, practicing relaxation techniques, exercising, reading some exciting fiction, listening to motivational tapes, and learning something we have never done before can help us develop as vital, dynamic, and well-rounded people [3].

**Wishing may be a great way to start, but conscious and active goal-setting will get you there faster.**

Learn to set goals for yourself. Setting goals reaffirms your sense of *I can*; it is an ackowledgment of your potential and capability. Unfortunately, many people rarely get beyond wishing, which lacks the power and commitment of setting a goal. Wishing may be a great way to start, but conscious and active goal-setting will get you there faster.

Be specific and concrete about your goals. Use numbers, names, and dates. Write out your goals—it strengthens your commitment, as well as the probability that you will realize them. Record them as if you have already achieved them, perhaps beginning with the words *I can* . . . Go back to your list from time to time to see how much you have accomplished. Continually update and revise your list with new goals.

If you are working in a particularly supportive environment, you may be getting a good bit of positive feedback about the work you are doing. Unfortunately, it is likely you do not get many strokes from the people you work with (who, incidentally, probably need them just as badly). So you need to learn to offer self-recognition and feedback. This behavior is a great way to practice focusing on the positive and will help you to perceive a failure or mistake as an impetus to set new goals for yourself.

To pat yourself on the back, use the same process my professor employed: look for what you did right. If you have ever found yourself lying awake in bed at night, agonizing over the bulletin board you have not changed in five months, over the papers you still have not graded, over the laundry you forgot to take out of the washer last Tuesday, you are a great candidate for this strategy.

Put a little datebook or a pen and pad next to the bed. Tonight and every night, before you shut your eyes, take a few seconds to make a list of at least three things you did right that day, regardless of the results or anyone else's reaction. The only rule is that you can't use the word *but*. Simply put down what you did well, what you tried for the first time, or what you feel good about . . . Even if it's only *my flag looked great!*

[1] Control issues, approval-seeking and rescuing are among the topics discussed in greater detail in Melody Beattie's *CoDependent No More*, (Hazelden Foundation. Central City, MN, 1987) as well as other resources on codependency. Although the term originated in work with families of alcholics, the dynamics of codependency can occur in any situation. Codependency is extremely common in teaching because of the nature of the profession.

[2] When you believe that another teacher's behavior is hampering student success, be cautious about interfereing. The more win-win your orientation becomes, the more aware you will be of other people's win-lose approaches. We all want to keep people from hurting one another, and it will be a matter of conscience at which point you become involved. Too often, however, it is just a judgment call: one person's teaching style is another person's hurtful behavior. That line can be pretty fine; I recommend extreme caution in getting involved.

[3] If you are feeling extremely stressed, depressed, stuck, or tempted to engage in negative or self-destructive behaviors, please consider joining a support group, talking to a counselor, or taking advantage of an employee assistance program if one exists. Find a place, preferably outside the realm of your immediate work world, where it is safe to explore and express your feelings, seek alternatives, and rethink your goals and directions.

# Appendix:
# Implications for
# administrators

For most of us, the word *discipline* conjures up thoughts of reactive and controlling measures for dealing with student misbehavior. However, the 21st century model of discipline proposed in this book is an ongoing, proactive set of behaviors used to create a cooperative environment which minimizes the likelihood of negative, disruptive behavior. (This positive discipline process can occur in any group—a classroom, department, building, or district.)

Consider yourself fortunate if you are working wih teachers who are already committed to a win-win discipline model, such as that described in this book. They will make your job much easier. These are teachers who assume responsibility for handling misbehaviors that occur in their classrooms. They will see you as a resource, not a rescuer, and will be far less likely to request that you solve their discipline problems for them. In contrast, teachers who use typical win-lose strategies frequently find those techniques frustrating and ineffective for managing conflicts with students, parents, or other teachers, and may frequently ask that you intervene.

Win-win teachers have more positive attitudes and are able to provide an atmosphere that encourages growth and learning. By focusing on the connections between choices and outcomes, these teachers help students to take responsibility for their actions and behaviors. As a result, their students are more likely to exhibit initiative, independence, self-management, and awareness of others' needs than students in a win-lose classroom, who often do only what is required to get by or act simply to avoid the teacher's criticism. Win-win teachers are also clear about their limits and boundaries, and secure enough to encourage empowerment among their students.

Yet 21st century discipline can be quite a challenge for any teacher unfamiliar with win-win management models. To generate their commitment, these teachers first need to learn how 21st century discipline can pay off for them. They will then need information about effective adult behaviors for achieving a variety of interactive goals. Your support will encourage these teachers to try new approaches and help build confidence in developing new techniques. It is important to realize that implementing successful techniques in the classroom takes much time and effort. A win-win focus involves relearning and retraining, and could take a teacher a number of years to fully implement.

The strategies described in this book also apply well to adult relationships. This may translate to *letting go* and sharing some of your power to involve teachers in decisions you may have previously made alone. Empowered teachers—those who feel they have input in decisions that affect them—are likely to commit enthusiastically to the success and welfare of the organization.

As an administrator, begin to think of new ways to motivate and empower your staff. The following are some examples:

- Give them opportunities to suggest topics and resources for in-services.
- Present options for scheduling, room assignment, or grade level.
- Try to accommodate staff members' needs for input and choice when making administrative decisions that concern them.
- Provide the most direct channels possible for access to supplies, resource personnel, and yourself.
- Offer acceptance, feedback, and support while

encouraging teachers to solve their problems.

- Visit every classroom to offer feedback, or just help out.
- Find something positive to say about every member of your staff.
- Make time each day to state verbal or written messages of recognition and appreciation.
- Encourage your staff to do the same for one another.
- Use motivators and rewards to show appreciation, recognize special achievements, or just break up routines.

As you model cooperative interactions with students, parents, and staff, you will set the tone for the entire school. The payoffs for you and the other adults in your building are considerable. But in terms of learning, behavior, and self-concept, the real winners are the students.

# About the author

Jane Bluestein has presented the information in this book, through workshops, to thousands of teachers and parents. She was formerly a classroom teacher with the Pittsburgh Public Schools, and has recently worked as a crisis-intervention counselor and teacher educator. She has appeared internationally as a speaker and talk-show guest, promoting positive adult-child relationships and interactions. Dr. Bluestein is author of *Being a Successful Teacher* and *Parents in a Pressure Cooker*, and has written for several magazines, including *Instructor*, *PTA Today*, and *McCall's*. She is president of Instructional Support Services of Albuquerque, New Mexico.

## INSTRUCTOR RESOURCE SERIES

**Big Idea Book** — 750 best classroom do-its and use-its from Instructor magazine. **IB401.**

**Big Basics Book** — 55 master plans for teaching the basics, with over 100 reproducibles. **IB402.**

**Big Holiday Book** — Seasonal songs, stories, poems, plays, and art, plus an activities calendar. **IB403.**

**Big Seasonal Arts & Crafts Book** — Over 300 projects for special days and seasons. **IB404.**

**Big Language Arts Book for Primary Grades** — 136 reading and language skills reproducibles. **IB405.**

**Big Math Book for Primary Grades** — 135 reproducibles on number concepts and processes. **IB406.**

**Big Book of Teacher Savers** — Class lists, letters to parents, record-keeping forms, calendars, maps, writing forms, and more. **IB407.**

**Synonyms, Sentences, and Spelling Bees: Language Skills Book A** — 140 reproducibles. **IB408.**

**Periods, Paragraphs, and Prepositions: Language Skills Book B** — Over 140 reproducibles. **IB409.**

**Big Book of Reading Ideas** — Teacher-tested reading ideas for use with any reading system. **IB410.**

**Teacher's Activity Calendar** — Red letter days, ideas, units for the school year. **IB411.**

**Early Education Almanac** — Hundreds of activities for kindergarten and beyond. **IB412.**

**Paper, Pen, and Think** — Ideas galore for developing a sequential writing program. **IB413.**

**Beating the Bulletin Board Blues** — Step-by-step ways to bulletin board learning centers. **IB414.**

**Success with Sticky Subjects** — Books A and B together offer over 240 reproducible worksheets for classroom drill in problem areas of the curriculum. **Book A—IB415. Book B—IB416.**

**Foolproof, Failsafe Seasonal Science** — Units, experiments, and quick activities. **IB417.**

**Poetry Place Anthology** — 605 favorite poems from Instructor, organized for instant access. **IB418.**

**Big Book of Plays** — 82 original, reproducible plays for all occasions and levels. **IB419.**

**Artfully Easy!** — "How-to" workshops on teaching art basics, group projects, and more! **IB420.**

**Big Book of Study Skills** — Techniques and activities for the basic subject areas. **IB421.**

**Big Book of Study Skills Reproducibles** — Over 125 classroom-tested worksheets for all levels. **IB422.**

**Big Book of Computer Activities** — A hands-on guide for using computers in every subject. **IB423.**

**Read-Aloud Anthology** — 98 stories for all grades and all occasions. **IB424.**

**Page-a-Day Pursuits** — Over 300 reproducibles on famous days, birthdays, and events. **IB425.**

**Big Book of Holiday Word Puzzles** — 400 skill-builders for 130 year 'round celebrations. **IB426.**

**Big Book of Health and Safety** — Reproducible activities to shape up the health curriculum. **IB427.**

**Teacher Savers Two** — Reproducible awards, contracts, letters, sanity-keepers galore. **IB428.**

**Celebrate America** — Over 200 reproducible activities about the symbols, the land, the people of the U.S.A. Maps, graphs, timelines, folklore, and more. Eight pull-out posters. **IB429.**

**Big Book of Absolutely Everything** — 1001 ideas to take you through the school year. **IB430.**

**Language Unlimited** — 160 reproducibles sharpen reading, writing, speaking, listening skills. **IB431.**

**Children and Media** — Activities help kids learn from TV, radio, film, videotape, print. **IB432.**

**Blockbuster Bulletin Boards** — 366 teacher originals for all grades, subjects, and seasons. **IB433.**

**Hey Gang! Let's Put On A Show** — 50 original skits, choral readings, plays for all ages. **IB434.**

**Puzzle Pals** — Mazes, decoders, wordsearches, hidden objects and more. **IB435.**

**Hands-On Science** — Jam-packed with facts and activities to develop young scientists, K-8. **IB436.**

**21st Century Discipline** — Practical strategies to teach students responsibility and self-control. **IB437.**

**Teaching Kids to Care** — 156 activities to help young children cooperate, share, and learn together. **IB250.**

**Games, Giggles, and Giant Steps** - 250 games for children ages 2-8; no equipment needed. **IB251**